ROBBE-GRILLET

Les Gommes *and* Le Voyeur

B.G. Garnham

Lecturer in French,
University of Durham

Grant & Cutler Ltd
1982

© Grant & Cutler Ltd
1982
ISBN 0 7293 0142 7

I.S.B.N. 84-499-6034-7

DEPÓSITO LEGAL: v. 2.669 - 1982

Printed in Spain by
Artes Gráficas Soler, S.A., Valencia
for
GRANT & CUTLER LTD
11 BUCKINGHAM STREET, LONDON W.C.2

Critical Guides to French Texts

19 R

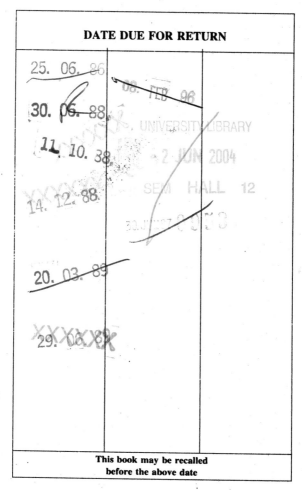

Critical Guides to French Texts

EDITED BY ROGER LITTLE, WOLFGANG VAN EMDEN, DAVID WILLIAMS

Contents

Prefatory Note

The organisation of this study of Robbe-Grillet's first two novels reflects my desire not to approach these novels in the way many critics have done, that is by establishing Robbe-Grillet's theoretical attitude to the novel and examining his works of fiction in the light of that. I thought it would be more fruitful to deal with the two texts first, trying to place myself in the position of 'general reader', and seeking to put them in a wider perspective in the final chapter. The first seven chapters correspond to what I feel the interests and queries of the general reader would be; these are examined in terms of the two texts, and then brought together in chapter 8.

As, at the time of writing, other editions are not available, references to *Les Gommes* and *Le Voyeur* are to the editions published by Les Editions de Minuit in 1953 and 1955.

Italicised numbers in parentheses, followed by page references, refer to the numbered items in the select bibliography at the end of this volume.

1. *Les Gommes:* the Detective Story

In his *Prière d'insérer* for the first edition of *Les Gommes* Robbe-Grillet describes the novel as follows:

> Il s'agit d'un événement précis, concret, essentiel: la mort d'un homme. C'est un événement à caractère policier — c'est-à-dire qu'il y a un assassin, un détective, une victime. En un sens, leurs rôles sont même respectés: l'assassin tire sur la victime, le détective résout la question, la victime meurt. Mais les relations qui les lient ne sont pas aussi simples, ou plutôt ne sont aussi simples qu'une fois le dernier chapitre terminé. Car le livre est justement le récit des vingt-quatre heures qui s'écoulent entre ce coup de pistolet et cette mort, le temps que la balle a mis pour parcourir trois ou quatre mètres — vingt-quatre heures "en trop".

Immediately the reader should be on his guard: behind the references to elements traditional to the detective story — murder, a detective, the solving of a mystery — lies a warning that all is not as it might at first appear to be. The central event is 'à caractère policier': it has something of the mystery thriller about it, but that is not all. The roles of the various characters are respected 'in a sense', but the relationships between them are not as straightforward as one might think. To some degree, of course, the reader's appetite is being whetted in the best publicity-writer's tradition, and Robbe-Grillet's mention in the last sentence of the twenty-four hours it takes for the bullet to find its mark adds an intriguing note; there is a promise of an ingenious story with a surprise ending, another example of a much appreciated genre. The warning, however, is of something more far-reaching than false trails and an unexpected dénouement: the events will be seen to have other characteristics, and the relationships between the characters will be more complex than those between victim, murderer and policeman. Above all, the twenty-four hours 'en trop' will take on a significance beyond that of the interval between two stages of a crime.

Nevertheless, the outward trappings of a detective story are there, carefully maintained and emphasised by the author. A clear forward impetus to the novel is provided by the efforts of the investigators to put together the various elements of the crime, and the reader is present at a procedure typical of the detective story: the attempted reconstruction of events, the creation of order out of disorder. The police and Wallas, the special agent, have come by information which is incomplete, contradictory and puzzling, and the reader, who is in something of a privileged position and knows more than they do, is a witness to their efforts to make sense of it; on this level the novel chronicles the progress of Wallas and Chief Inspector Laurent through the maze of evidence, reports and hypotheses which are inevitably part of the investigation of a crime. The reader can enjoy many ironies as Wallas and Laurent create different forms of order, none of which corresponds to the order that he, the reader, knows; he will, however, become part of the greater irony as he finds doubt and uncertainty cast over what he took that order to be.

Wallas, the special agent, has been sent to the unnamed provincial city to investigate the reported murder of Daniel Dupont, an economics professor. Unknown to him, as it is to the local police, Dupont has been only wounded, and is taking refuge in the clinic of Dr Juard; his 'death' has been announced, with the connivance of authorities in the capital, in order to mislead those responsible for the crime. Dupont, it appears, is the latest victim of a gang of terrorists, whose plan is to assassinate various influential individuals; all the crimes are timed to take place at 7.30 p.m. Garinati, the would-be assassin on this occasion, acting on the instructions of his leader, Bona, had gained access to Dupont's house, but, because of his own incompetence, had failed in his mission; he now seeks out Wallas, in order to watch him, but arrives after Wallas has left his room at the rather seedy café near the scene of the crime.

These details are provided in the prologue, which, as well as setting the scene in this way, skilfully creates an atmosphere of uncertainty and ambivalence which Robbe-Grillet will later exploit to great advantage. In these early pages, the uncertainty and ambivalence are consonant with the atmosphere of a detective story: the café proprietor is sceptical about the death, finding it unreasonable that the victim should die when Anna, the servant, had declared that he had been only slightly wounded in the arm; Garinati is convinced that Dupont could not have died from his shot, and plans to return to the house the following day to finish the job; Chief Inspector Laurent has been instructed not to proceed with investigations, and has been told that the body has already been removed, so that for him the case is closed. Appearance and reality, then, are in their familiar stances of opposition. Dupont and Juard, of course, know the 'truth', but are actively engaged in disguising it, and the other characters each have a limited perspective of it and fail properly to grasp it. It is in these circumstances that Wallas arrives to begin his investigation.

From the very beginning Robbe-Grillet shows that he is at home in the detective story and that he is well equipped to put its essential characteristics to good use. Not merely, however, to tell an ingenious tale, but to investigate questions of the individual's perceptions of reality and the nature and function of the novel itself. With a central character whose enquiries leave him constantly perplexed as to the significance of events, and with its multiple hypotheses and versions of the crime — a crime which properly speaking does not exist, since it is finally committed only at the end of the book — *Les Gommes* accentuates the mysterious nature of reality, which is distorted every time it is described. Like the disparate information available to Wallas, which comes to him in the wrong order, as it were, and with the connecting elements missing, reality is susceptible to multiple interpretations, and is perceived not as it is, but as each individual would like to perceive it. Valerie Minogue speaks of the 'equilibrium of possibilities' in the novel (*12*, p.432): reality has been replaced by a series of realities, each subjectively perceived and each of equal validity. In the prologue (p.37) the pieces of débris in the canal can be seen in any number of ways — as a clown's face, as a mythological beast, or as a map of America — and none is any more 'real' or 'true' than any other. Further, the detective story, emphasising as it does the prime role of the puzzle, arouses in the reader the anticipation that the puzzle will be solved, that out of disorder order will eventually come. The reader expects to proceed from uncertainty to knowledge, and it is that expectation which Robbe-Grillet will frustrate; he will deny the reader's need for intelligibility, for a satisfying, ordered whole, and in so doing, he will throw into question some of the bases on which the traditional novel rests.

In order to achieve these ends, it is important for Robbe-Grillet to make those elements of the detective story which figure in *Les Gommes* persuasive. *Les Gommes* is not, as some critics have suggested, a parody, but rather a novel in which the reader, familiar with the genre, is lulled into a false sense of security. He is taken along a path which is enticing, through territory which is generally well known; Robbe-Grillet will, however, undermine the foundations gradually, so that the suspicions of his reader are not awakened too abruptly, and will be all the more persistent for that.

Many of the conventions governing this sort of enterprise are respected. Wallas sets out on his search for information, and questions those likely to possess relevant knowledge, such as Anna the servant, Mme Bax, Dr Juard and Dupont's wife. His investigations are complemented by those of the police, who examine particularly the possibilities of suicide (a favourite theory of Laurent) or murder by an illegitimate son of Dupont (based on 'evidence' given by the concierge and the café proprietor to a zealous inspector). Together Wallas and Laurent question Post Office employees about the mysterious activities of André VS, who figures as a possible suspect. Traditional significance is given to fingerprints, footprints and ballistics. There are political overtones to the affair, with Bona and his gang of systematic assassins and Roy-Dauzet, the minister, and the authorities in the capital. In the shadows lurks the fanciful figure of Fabius, celebrated head of the Bureau des Enquêtes, whose fixation with the measurements of agents' foreheads is sombrely recalled by Wallas (pp.163 sqq.). In accepted fashion, Laurent suddenly arrives at the revelation of the truth (p.245); it is a truth he communicates to Wallas a moment too late, a moment after Wallas, who has entered Dupont's house to lie in wait for the assassin, has himself killed Dupont, who has returned to collect some important documents.

Wallas thus becomes the murderer; the interval of twenty-four hours between the first shot and the death is explained, and the detective story has its 'surprise' ending. Yet to the attentive reader, the ending is not a surprise, and in this regard — the culpability of Wallas — Robbe-Grillet undertakes that undermining of the foundations which is central to his purpose. Wallas fires the fatal shot on page 252, but in fact he has taken on the persona of the murderer long before that. Suspicions are first overtly stated on page 76, albeit lightheartedly, when Laurent points out that Wallas has recently come to the city, has stayed near the scene of the crime, and that his arrival has not been declared to the police; Laurent adds, in answer to Wallas's protests, 'Les bons assassins n'ont-ils pas toujours un alibi?', and ironically, at the end of the novel, the train ticket, which would establish the time of his arrival, is missing (p.260). Laurent also notices that Wallas's gun, the same calibre as that of Dupont's assailant, has one bullet missing. Following Madame Bax's description of the man she saw tampering with the bell mechanism at Dupont's gate, Wallas is 'recognised' by the drunkard, who had also witnessed the scene, and Wallas, in an apparently imaginary episode, is presented in the role of the man at the gate. He is later 'identified' as the man who has collected letters addressed to André VS at the *poste restante*, and throughout the novel he is likened not only to this possible assassin, but also to Garinati, and indeed our first view of Wallas (p.45) is of him in a position identical to that of Garinati a few pages earlier (p.20), leaning over the rail of the bridge. Similarities between the two men are increasingly stressed. On page 24, in a scene apparently depicting Garinati's entrance into the house, one finds the sentence: 'Un autre, ici-même, pensant le poids de chacun de ses pas, viendrait...'; the same words are repeated and amplified on page 41. On page 99 Wallas seems to have taken Garinati's place: 'Non! Il est impossible de confondre plus longtemps Garinati avec cette fiction: un autre dès ce soir devra le remplacer dans sa tâche', and on page 103 Bona states 'Ce soir, c'est l'affaire d'un autre'.

B.F. Stoltzfus has noted the significance: 'Unlike the real whodunit in which a murder occurs at the beginning and the reader is kept in suspense until the resolution of guilt and innocence, the murder in *Les Gommes* occurs at the end. It is the murder itself which casts light on the activities of the detective, rather than vice-versa' (*19*, p.69). Wallas, the murderer at the end, is also the murderer at the beginning: details given at different moments in the novel to implicate him, or to arouse suspicions about him, are not simply clues a devious author is offering to an observant reader; they are means by which traditional chronology is destroyed. Robbe-Grillet has taken the 'conclusion' — that Wallas is led to kill Dupont at the end of the book — but instead of merely making that conclusion emerge from preceding circumstances, he introduces it into the body of the novel. Bruce Morrissette remarks upon the reader's doubts: 'vers le milieu du roman, on commence à se douter que les renseignements "complets" fournis au lecteur sur la situation de Wallas et de Dupont recouvrent un mystère qui va s'épaississant. Le lecteur, qui jusqu'alors suivait les efforts d'un groupe de personnes cherchant à découvrir ce que lui, lecteur, sait déjà, s'attache désormais aux errements d'un homme attiré dans une voie obscure vers un dénouement encore insoupçonné' (*13*, p.46). It can be debated whether the dénouement is unexpected, just as one might dissent from B.F. Stoltzfus's comment that 'the irony of the novel is that Wallas thinks himself innocent until his guilt is brought to consciousness, a revelation which is surprising to the reader as it is to Wallas' (*19*, p.69). Certainly it is some time before Wallas's guilt is brought to consciousness, for he has many kilometres to walk through the city and many questions to ask before the crime is solved, but Robbe-Grillet is skilful enough to introduce into the novel a sense of that guilt, notably in the scenes where Wallas becomes involved in a tortuous conversation with a woman in the street (p.54) and where he asks a policeman for direction (p.135). On both occasions he is forced into a false position by his reluctance to explain honestly his intentions; he has to invent new contexts to justify himself and seems constantly obliged to account for his actions: 'Quel mauvais sort le force donc, aujourd'hui, à donner des raisons partout sur son passage?' (p.136). In the mind of the reader Wallas is not only a confused investigator, but a dissimulator as well.

As Stoltzfus says, the murder casts light on the activities of Wallas, and also on his character; it is the final expression of what has always been present in him. The detective story has offered one puzzle — the circumstances surrounding the attempted murder of Dupont — and on to the uncertainties which that puzzle affords Robbe-Grillet has grafted other uncertainties, of which the most notable is that of time. Wallas's watch stops at 7.30, the time of the first murder attempt, and starts again the moment he kills Dupont. Twenty-four hours have passed unrecorded; chronological time has been suspended, and the first and second shots fired become identical. The 'real' twenty-four hours — the time in which the events of the detective story take place — are replaced by the 'human' time-scale of Wallas, which is outside chronology; the circumstances which bring him to commit murder, it is suggested, are deep within him, in his doubts, obsessions and memories. Since they are not the product of time, the primacy of the clock must be challenged: Wallas is not merely the murderer when he squeezes the trigger, but throughout the book.

From the beginning of the novel, when the reader is warned that 'Bientôt malheureusement le temps ne sera plus le maître' (p.11), chronological time is undermined and the 'vingt-quatre heures en trop' are in fact annulled. Antoine, confusing the first names of two victims, anticipates on Tuesday morning a crime which will be known only the following day. Conversely, Anna, the servant, confuses the days and states that it is Monday; she is corrected only timidly by Wallas, as if he himself is in some doubt. Tuesday has 'disappeared', and the murder of Daniel Dupont, which is announced on that day, is not authentic: his death is officially declared, but false; for Laurent it is as if no crime has been committed at all, and Wallas will eventually commit the crime under investigation.

Hypotheses concerning the murder may be made true or false because of the dislocation of time: the café proprietor is right to say that Dupont cannot have died 'si vite', and Antoine is right to claim that Albert Dupont is a victim of the terrorists. Laurent is justified in his suggestion that two assassins are involved, in that both Garinati and Wallas will fire shots, at the beginning and end of the novel, and in a sense his theory of Dupont's suicide is justified, since, at the end of the novel, Dupont's behaviour, strongly influenced by an over-active imagination, convincing him that the assassin is awaiting him, directly contributes to his death. These hypotheses are correct in essence, but are inappropriate at the moment they are expressed; they are out of step with the chronological development of the plot, but achieve their full significance in a timeless context.

Thus the enigma of the detective story has been adapted by Robbe-Grillet to other ends. The traditional enigma ('Who is the murderer?' or, 'The murderer being known, what were his motives?') depends upon the existence of a secret, known to the author and, through the activities of his characters, revealed to the reader. The solution is not in itself mysterious, since it is formulated by the author; it is absent from the work and unknown to the reader until the appropriate moment, although indications of it, echoes or suggestions of it may be introduced into the narrative at earlier stages. The reader progresses, dependent upon the good-will of the author and the greater or lesser degree to which he remains secretive, to the divulging of a preconceived truth, which, in the first instance, the author has disguised. The importance of the omniscient narrator — the privileged viewpoint, the all-seeing eye — is crucial: he organises the material and imparts meaning to it. He possesses the code which the reader must break.

In *Les Gommes* Robbe-Grillet has taken this genre and changed its emphasis. Now the text is not a progression towards the solution of an enigma; the text and the solution are one and the same. The elements necessary to an understanding of the events of the novel are built directly into the text; instead of a solution absent from the work, the author presents everything immediately. A hidden mystery has been replaced by what Dina Dreyfus, in an enlightening article, calls 'un mystère en pleine lumière' (*8*, p.274); the elements of the narrative may well be puzzling, and subject to different interpretations, susceptible of diverse combinations, but they are all present, and the text itself takes on a necessity, a self-sufficiency. Robbe-Grillet has weakened the authority of the omniscient narrator, and placed a much greater responsibility upon the shoulders of his reader, who becomes a creator rather than a spectator. The reader has to create the story of Wallas and the murder of Dupont from the material presented to him, material which above all does not lend itself to one single meaning. In this way the enigma of the detective story gives way to several enigmas, the solution to which is in the responsiveness and creativity of the reader. This is true not only of the identity of the murderer (where details are at their most obvious), but also of Wallas's character and motivation. Here, as we shall see in subsequent chapters of this study, Robbe-Grillet has opened several avenues of possibility. He is intent upon removing from the plot of the novel what he calls its tranquillity and its certainty. What better way to bring home to the reader his ideas than the undermining of a genre which traditionally depends upon a tightly constructed plot?

2. *Les Gommes:* the Temptations of Mythology

The mythological infrastructure of *Les Gommes* has been well noted by critics, particularly by Bruce Morrissette. Opinions as to the purpose and significance of this infrastructure, however, are varied; some critics see the novel as a modern version of the Oedipus story (either as adaptation or parody), and openly declare that Wallas's behaviour makes sense only if interpreted in terms of an Oedipus complex, while others, notably Olga Bernal, see the novel as one satirising the predilection of modern authors to base their stories on ancient myths. L.S. Roudiez finds that Robbe-Grillet uses the myth 'as a backdrop for a contemporary plot that seems to have no direct connection to the older legend' (*16*, p.80) and elsewhere offers the view that 'the references to the Oedipus myth were inserted with the deliberate purpose of having the reader join the group of mythomaniacs in the text' (*17*, p.209). B.F. Stoltzfus states that through the myth Robbe-Grillet can show how Wallas's actions are eventually controlled by fate (*19*, p.73), a view shared by John Sturrock, who considers Wallas to be a free agent subjected to a pressure, the Oedipus myth, which he cannot resist (*21*, p.174).

The diversity of these opinions is not surprising, when one considers the manner in which classical allusions are introduced into the novel. Some are overt, even unsubtle, some are oblique and others are obscure; one senses on some occasions a playfulness on the part of the author and an enjoyment in the possible mystification of his reader. It would certainly be hard to deny that a series of mythological references exists, but the question as to whether they amount to a systematic and meaningful pattern is not easy to answer.

In its most widely known form, the myth of Oedipus has three main elements: first, after his abandonment in childhood, the murder by Oedipus of his father and his marriage to his mother; second, his search for the truth concerning his father's death and the discovery of his own guilt; third, his punishment and exile. In his use of the myth in *Les Gommes* Robbe-Grillet is highly selective, since of these three elements only the second is clearly exploited. Wallas is a plausible reincarnation of Oedipus in that, searching for a murderer, he discovers that the murderer is himself. He makes that discovery not by any return to the past, but by committing the very act in question; he does not reinterpret an act already accomplished, but assumes a role. The third element in the myth, noted above, does not seem applicable here. Wallas is not punished, and, as more than one critic has (*like Matthews*) pointed out, if he is Oedipus, he is an Oedipus who gets away with it. He is on his first assignment as a special agent; he is thus on trial, and since the investigation has not been a notable success, it seems probable that he will be transferred to another division, a fate only the most lively imagination could equate with self-inflicted blindness and exile.

The remaining element — the relationship between Oedipus and his parents — is, in terms of *Les Gommes*, much more problematic. It is in respect of this that critics are most divided, anxious to see or determined to reject in the novel a post-Freudian interpretation of the myth as hostility to the father in view of desire for the mother. Robbe-Grillet offers scope for debate, but, as might be expected, no answers. There are several references which are apparently relevant: at different moments as he wanders through the city, Wallas is stirred by memories of an earlier visit he made there with his mother, and he eventually remembers that it was in search of his father (p.239). The image repeatedly associated with that visit is that of 'un canal en cul-de-sac', and on page 49 Wallas notes 'un canal, immobile en apparence, couloir rectiligne laissé par les hommes au lac natal'. A little later (p.64) he walks along the water's edge, 'attiré, soutenu par elle', and it may well be that Robbe-Grillet is deliberately using somewhat traditional symbolism of journeys from and to the womb. He enters a stationery shop kept by the woman who is, apparently, Dupont's wife, and, as on other such occasions, his search for an india-rubber is accompanied by a note of discreet eroticism: the woman's 'petit rire de gorge' (p.131) will remain with him.

Such Oedipus elements are accompanied by other echoes. Wallas notes the design on curtains at windows he passes: '... un sujet allégorique de grande série: bergers recueillant un enfant abandonné, ou quelque chose dans ce genre-là' (p.50); there are several references to the phrase 'enfant trouvé'. Throughout the novel Wallas is harrassed by the drunkard with his riddles, one of which seems particularly appropriate to Oedipus: 'Quel est l'animal qui est parricide le matin, inceste à midi et aveugle le soir?' (p.234), and at the end Wallas can sit and contemplate his swollen feet. There are references to Thebes and Corinth, and the Post Office, with its mysterious messages, has something about it of the Delphic oracle. A statuette (p.217) depicts an old blind man led by a child, and momentarily the debris in the canal takes on the form of the Sphinx (p.37). The middle two letters of six in the brand-name of the desired india-rubber are DI, and Wallas's act of murder is anticipated by the inspector's theory of a long-lost son.

What does all this add up to? Are we to sympathise with Leo Bersani's rather sour remark, '...when we have read Bruce Morrissette's depressingly convincing enumeration of the Oedipus symbols and references in the novel, the only inventiveness left is of the objectionable sort that consists in the writer's cleverly camouflaging the archetypal ideas that are his main interest' (*6*, p.309)? Or with Stoltzfus's view that 'Robbe-Grillet has given us the literary equivalent of a Freudian interpretation of the Oedipus myth' (*19*, p.75)? Is the novel to be interpreted in terms of the myth, or, as some would have it, in spite of it? Is the myth central to the novel or irrelevant? Certainly the references to the Oedipus myth are not to be denied, and lest we should be tempted to dismiss them, the author has set them in a context with a generally 'classical' atmosphere. The statue in the Place de la Préfecture (pp.62, 85) is that of a Greek chariot, possibly that of Laius, Oedipus's father; the name of the sculptor at the base, V. Daulis, contains an anagram of Laius. To Wallas in his search, the city takes on the appearance of a labyrinth, and there are seemingly gratuitous references to 'les tentacules d'une méduse géante' (p.122) and to 'un gigantesque oracle, magnifique, indéchiffrable et terrifiant' (p.208). The

novel itself is organised into five chapters, with prologue and
epilogue, reminiscent of classical tragedy, and into the middle of
a conversation between Laurent and Marchat, the businessman,
Robbe-Grillet slips the phrase 'une *erreur*, une tragique erreur'
(p.153). References to Bona and his terrorist organisation — 'Et
les autres que Garinati ne connaît pas, toute l'Organisation
autour de Bona, au-dessus même, cette immense machine...'
(p.39) — are reminiscent of Cocteau's *La Machine infernale*,
itself a version of the Oedipus legend.

What is clear is that Robbe-Grillet is not retelling the mythical
story. He does not give anything like a complete version of it,
nor does he seek to reinterpret it. He is not using it to throw light
upon it, and does not exploit the fundamental themes which the
myth embraces. This is not a novel in which sexual desires and
parent-child relationships are explored in any profound sense.
If, to take the case at its most extreme, Wallas kills his father
(Dupont) because of his desire for his mother (Evelyne Dupont),
the reader is not given anything but the most general indication
of what constitutes his passion. This is largely accounted for by
Robbe-Grillet's rejection of explanatory psychology (to be
discussed later); however, even allowing for the author's refusal
to analyse Wallas and his desire to project his mental state in images before the reader, the substance of the myth is missing. We
have external details; we are regularly reminded that Wallas's
actions may well have their precedents and that the pattern of his
behaviour is not an original one. What we lack is the integration
of the present and the past. The myth is a distant shadow, an
unsettling, even teasing undercurrent, and here, perhaps, lies its
true significance.

Through the myth (and by association, classical tragedy)
Robbe-Grillet can introduce the idea of order, continuity and
necessity. While the detective story in *Les Gommes* is the scene
of doubt, uncertainty and a multiplicity of explanations and
theories, the myth offers the perspective of necessity and certainty. The detective story, with its endless possibilities and prospect
of change is the antithesis of a tragedy, with its emphasis on har-
mony, unity and the orderly unfolding of inevitable events. The
myth corresponds, it would appear, to that part of Wallas which

seeks order: 'C'est volontairement qu'il marche vers un avenir inévitable et parfait. Autrefois il lui est arrivé trop souvent de se laisser prendre aux cercles du doute et de l'impuissance, maintenant il marche; il a retrouvé là sa durée' (p.52). He is seeking to progress in a straight line (as opposed to his wanderings in the city, constantly finding himself on the Boulevard Circulaire), with movements which are precise, mechanical and necessary; there is a foreshadowing of this in the scene depicting Garinati's entrance into Dupont's house: 'Celui qui s'avance ainsi, dans le secret, pour exécuter l'ordre, ne connaît ni la peur, ni le doute. Il ne sent plus le poids de son propre corps. Ses pas sont silencieux comme ceux du prêtre; ils glissent sur le tapis et sur les dalles, aussi réguliers, aussi impersonnels, aussi définitifs. La ligne droite est le plus court chemin d'un point à l'autre' (p.23).

The myth, for Robbe-Grillet, represents not the supernatural, not the irrational, but the inevitable. He uses it to introduce the idea of fate. The killing of Dupont by Wallas is 'son oeuvre d'inéluctable justice' (p.41); he feels he has fallen into a trap (p.90) and that he is led by fate: 'Quel mauvais sort le force donc, aujourd'hui, à donner des raisons partout sur son passage?' (p.136). As the decisive moment approaches, a phrase repeatedly comes to his lips: 'il va falloir...' (p.185). Here is an echo of the order which reigns on the very first page, before it is destroyed by the events of the day, 'enveloppés de leur cerne d'erreur et de doute', events which soon set about their task, which is to 'introduire çà et là, sournoisement, une inversion, un décalage, une confusion, une courbature...' (p.11).

The myth is attractive, but it is also dangerous. Unlike the Wallas of the detective story, who wanders in a labyrinth, conscious of the *invraisemblance* of the events he is caught up in, the Wallas of the myth is in a context of order and necessity; but this is a context which, despite his efforts, robs him of his freedom and individuality. In this way the myth and the detective story in *Les Gommes* pull against each other, effecting a subtle form of 'gommage', whereby the potential significance, or order, suggested by one is cancelled, or erased, by the network of meanings associated with the other. This 'gommage' is further demonstrated by the scene in the window of the stationery shop (p.131). The display represents an artist painting a ruined Greek temple (later identified as the ruins of Thebes), but standing before a large photograph of a modern house (the scene of the crime). The photograph is so striking that it is seen as 'la négation du dessin censé le reproduire', and when the scene recurs (p.177) the painting and the subject have been reversed: now the artist stands before a Greek temple, but his painting is that of the house. Roudiez interprets this as the victory of one over the other: 'The implication seems clear: the myth of Oedipus is negated by the plot of *Les Gommes*. More generally, myth fails as an attempt to explain reality and is denied by reality' (*16*, p.83).

Such a dismissal of myth would be consonant with Robbe-Grillet's statements (in *Pour un nouveau roman*) rejecting 'les vieux mythes de la profondeur' (*1*, p.22) and the 'univers entièrement tragifié' (*1*, p.60) of such writers as Sartre and Camus. It could be taken to express Robbe-Grillet's challenge to the notion of a 'tragic complicity' between man and the world. In this line of argument the myth would be seen as destructive, leading the reader down a series of false trails, presenting him with misinterpretations and fallacies which feed upon his desire for intelligibility. The reader would thus be brought to book for his failure to adopt a sceptical stance towards that part of his cultural heritage which is built upon an acceptance of myths which falsify his vision of reality. To press home his case, Roudiez adopts a sensible, practical approach, emphasising incompleteness in the novel: he points out that Wallas does not solve the drunkard's riddles and does not seduce or marry Dupont's wife; as a child he came to the city to seek his father and did not originate there, and in any event the theory of the victim's son seems to be the result primarily of an inspector's over-active imagination.

These arguments notwithstanding, one remains uneasy: to relegate myth to the position of a 'distortion of reality' and to argue that it has been introduced into the novel in order to mislead the reader is to undervalue an element which has considerable and more positive significance. Fate, as we have said, comes with the myth to challenge the arbitrariness of the detective story, an arbitrariness which is itself heightened by Robbe-Grillet's ironic use of the genre. The myth's value lies not in its illusory nature, nor in its formal neatness, not in its ultimate 'meaning', but in the alternative pattern it represents. It offers a counterbalancing system to that of the plot, another way of arranging events. What constitutes fate — the will of the gods, the uncontrollable factors of human personality, the inexplicable conjunction of events — is not the concern of Robbe-Grillet. He is not intent upon making a statement upon the nature and extent of free-will, but a statement which is fundamentally a literary one. If one of the two elements in contention, myth and reality, is negated by the other, then that other is reaffirmed and strengthened; but if they are both of equal weight and authority, then each is challenged in its turn. By the very design of the novel, Robbe-Grillet has made it impossible to identify clearly Wallas with Oedipus; by the distortions he has operated within the detective story, he has made him other than a conventional special agent. Neither aspect can account wholly for *Les Gommes*, which is the result — at least partly — of the tension between the two. As was pointed out at the end of the first chapter, Robbe-Grillet seeks to undermine the authority of plot; the myth plays its part in this undermining by offering an alternative register. It may well offer with it a certain mocking laugh on the part of the author, for the references to Oedipus are profuse enough to suggest a coherent pattern, but elusive enough to refuse that pattern.

3. *Les Gommes*: Objects — Perception and Usage

It is with regard to his description of objects that Robbe-Grillet has gained notoriety. Many critics, irritated or bemused by lengthy passages in which objects are seen in terms of their measurements, surface appearance and special relationships one with another, have accused him of 'dehumanizing' the novel and filling it with inert matter. For many, an absence of psychological analysis seemed to bring an impoverishment in terms of character-study which was compounded by the profusion of minutely observed objects; these objects, given no depth or meaning, had an insistent presence and an immobility which threatened to take all life from the novel. They had no immediately obvious relationship with the action and contributed no further level of meaning to the events described. The legend of Robbe-Grillet *chosiste* was born, encouraged, it must be said, by the sympathetic criticism of Roland Barthes.

Les Gommes has a good measure of such descriptions, and there are many examples of what Robbe-Grillet signals in *Pour un nouveau roman* as '...l'adjectif optique, descriptif, celui qui se contente de mesurer, de situer, de limiter...' (*1*, p.23); what is described is represented only in terms of its surface appearance, as in the scenes of the city as Wallas wanders through it, with notably the bridge and its mechanism. There is also the description, which rapidly became famous, of the quarter tomato which Wallas comes upon in a restaurant (p.161), where in a passage of fifteen lines, which has ostensibly no connection with what precedes and follows it, an 'objective' view of the fruit is given in terms of its shape, colour and texture.

Such descriptions as these emphasise the view that the only quality of the external world is its presence. It hides beneath its surface no meaning, no life, and above all it enters into no communion with man: 'Or le monde n'est ni signifiant ni absurde. Il *est* tout simplement' (*1*, p.18). It is part of the new novel's role to 'decondition' the reader, to enable him to see the world about him with new eyes and to undo the work of what Robbe-Grillet calls 'des franges de culture (psychologie, morale, métaphysique etc.)' which have deformed objects, making them more familiar and reassuring by tainting them with human emotions and meanings. The pathetic fallacy in literature has wedded man and the world in a false union and made the latter, in Robbe-Grillet's words, 'le vague reflet de l'âme vague du héros, l'image de ses tourments, l'ombre de ses désirs' (*1*, p.20). The new novel should reinstate the world in its true condition, existing independently of man; man must curb his desire to appropriate the world, to draw it closer to himself by deforming it with meaning.

Because the descriptions of objects in the novel offer no comforting explanations or reassuring complicity, they heighten the mysterious atmosphere and introduce elements of discontinuity, or dislocation, to the narrative. The material world, in its insistent presence, stands as a counterpoint to human attempts to give order and meaning to disparate events; Wallas is moving in a world where the streets of the city do not lead to the desired destination, and it is also a world where the objects seem at every turn to be about to outstrip the human consciousness which seeks to encompass them. The quarter tomato's presence is explicable — it is part of the processed food offered for human consumption in a restaurant — and yet it takes on a curious independence because, although it falls within Wallas's perspective, it is described in terms which seem to exclude that perspective and the human consciousness which is part of it. The quarter tomato becomes strangely disturbing; it has no obvious function, just as the india-rubbers which Wallas seeks have no obvious function. On four occasions (pp.65, 132, 177 and 239) Wallas enters a stationery shop in search of a particular type of rubber, and there are fleeting references to others (pp.66, 77). Such persistence is unexplained, and the reader has no further information concerning Wallas's character to which he could relate this particular behaviour. Wallas has no characteristics of the traditional sort: the reader is given no details of his past, his family connections, his attitudes to life in general. There is no physical description of him; he does not exist beyond his actions and perceptions as they are recounted, and all the reader knows of him, or cares to speculate about him, is to be constructed from the pictures within the pages of the novel. The search of the india-rubbers seems extraneous to other concerns of the novel and as such is a striking example of that dislocation mentioned above.

Such techniques might seem to confirm the fears of dubious critics, steeling themselves to face the entrance of the slide-rule and the catalogue into literature. The door would appear to be open to the worst excesses of *chosisme* and to an 'objective' literature which, in abandoning traditional virtues, has little to offer but a sterile precision. In this connection the word 'camera' has sprung to the lips of many, who have chosen to ignore that a camera, since it is in the hands of a photographer, is selective and interpretative. Robbe-Grillet himself is quick to point out that total impersonality in description is impossible, and he insists on many occasions that his novels are subjective in that what is described is perceived by someone: the world exists through the human gaze.

Remarks such as these give an indication of a second purpose of descriptions in *Les Gommes*, one which comes to modify the first. While it is true that the world, for Robbe-Grillet, exists without any significance beyond its existence, the human consciousness can be defined only in terms of its perception of something other than itself. That is the limit of the relationship between man and the world: there is no communion, no complicity, but an identification of one by the other. The identification does not take place in the absolute: the individual consciousness does not take stock of the entire world, but part of it, and in its selectivity reveals more of itself than of the world. Robbe-Grillet allows that, for brief moments at least, objects may become what he calls 'un support aux passions humaines', but is quick to add: '...elles [les choses] n'accepteront la tyrannie des significations qu'en apparence — comme par dérision — pour mieux montrer à quel point elles restent étrangères à l'homme' (*1*, p.20).

Anxious as he is to avoid traditional character-analysis, Robbe-Grillet seeks to *create* a state of mind by projecting it into

images. He will not comment upon the content of a consciousness, but describes it, leaving to the reader the work of interpretation. On every page the reader is faced not with what the
characters think or feel, but with what they see — in, of course,
the widest sense: they see literally what is before them and they
see also with their mind's eye. The novel constantly moves between the immediacy of the scene in the present — in the Café des
Alliés, in the Post Office, beside the canal and so on — and the
scene in the mind of the character, which will consist of
memories, fantasies and imaginings. That scene in the mind will
be as immediate and as urgent as the other, the scene before the
eyes; it is, like the other, lived in the present, for the mind knows
no other tense. It can certainly distinguish what was from what
is or what might be, but it experiences them all in the present.

In this way the descriptions of objects take on in the novel a
second function, distinct from that of accentuating a distance
between man and the world, and indeed contradictory to it. The
india-rubbers are important because they are perceived by
Wallas. Robbe-Grillet gives no clear information, of course, and
the reader is left to speculate, but it may well be that in them lie
clues to Wallas's character. His very persistence in seeking the
india-rubber may well denote an obsessive nature. In the first
two instances, the search is associated with a wave of erotic
desire; in their quality of erasure and self-erasure, the rubbers
may represent a wish on the part of Wallas to deny his present
situation or even to destroy himself. The adjectives applied to
them ('friable', p.66; 'douce, légère, friable...', p.132) may suggest qualities in Wallas himself; the reader notes the contrast
between these adjectives and the description of the paperweight
in Dupont's house (representing perhaps Dupont himself), a
description (p.26) transformed on page 244, immediately prior
to the murder, into 'le cube de pierre vitrifiée aux arêtes, aux
coins meurtriers'.

In this way objects become the reflection of characters' feel-
ings or situation; they are a visual interpretation of them. On
page 217 Garinati's uncertainties are portrayed in terms of the
displacement of objects on a mantlepiece; the barely perceptible
flaw in the quarter tomato (p.161) may suggest a flaw in Wallas,

a further indication that he is not all that he first appears to be. At the beginning and at the end of the novel, the café proprietor is seen not only in terms of his actions in his establishment, but also in terms of his reflection in a mirror above the counter and a further reflection in the glass door; the multiple images of the man, and the deformation of his appearance, making it seem as if he is in an aquarium with associated, threatening images of shapes and fantoms (pp.12, 15, 264), afford possible interpretations, or correlatives, of his character — his impenetrability, his mysterious past (further suggested by the untimely death of Pauline and 'le rebut de cinquante années d'existence mal digérée' (p.16)) and his uncertainty: the multiple images of 'le patron, le patron...' (p.12) are echoed by the man's own words at the end of the novel, as he seeks to affirm his own identity: 'Le patron, c'est moi. Le patron c'est moi. Le patron c'est moi le patron ... le patron... le patron...' (p.263). These images also serve to accentuate the confusion between appearance and 'reality' and provide a warning to the reader that he must not trust in appearance — one of a series of warnings throughout the novel which are discussed in the next chapter of this study.

In the projection into images of the characters' 'inner film' Robbe-Grillet's approach is at its most oblique and at times tends towards that playfulness which can be detected in his use of the Oedipus myth. The novel further suffers in this respect from the lack of a single perspective and from an uneasy balance between the characters' viewpoint and a narrator's voice; moreover Robbe-Grillet is not entirely consistent, since in his depiction of character he does not always entirely manage to avoid the temptations of traditional interior monologue. Nonetheless the reader is given ample evidence that Robbe-Grillet's purpose is not that of providing an 'objective' account of the material world, that is to reproduce it 'scientifically', but to represent it in its ambivalent relationship with the human consciousness. There is at work what Robbe-Grillet, giving one possible significance to the title of the novel, calls 'un double mouvement de création et de gommage' (*I*, p.127) and 'ce même mouvement paradoxal (construire en détruisant)' (*I*, p.130). Descriptions of the material world, while affirming its presence, reject any idea of ultimate meaning; that idea must be erased from the novel, just as the quarter tomato in *Les Gommes* erases any idea of a referential model of a 'real' tomato, by which it is to be judged. The importance of the quarter tomato lies not in the 'accuracy' of its description, but in its role within the context of the novel itself; the descriptions of the city in *Les Gommes* are not included in order to provide a realistic background, but to provide visual correlatives of the characters' dilemmas.

Techniques of description as they are used in *Les Gommes* are challenging. A reader with preferences for the virtues of traditional techniques will certainly be stirred by the demands made upon him, for Robbe-Grillet has notably exploited that essential quality of immediacy of the image, but that same reader might be justified in feeling that the author has not exploited his ideas and his talents to the full; he might suspect that Robbe-Grillet is engaged less upon demonstration than upon enquiry, enquiry into the literary process as a whole, and that must be the subject of the final chapter of this study on *Les Gommes*.

4. *Les Gommes:* 'Le roman d'un roman qui ne se fait pas'

In his preface to Nathalie Sarraute's novel *Portrait d'un inconnu*, published in 1948, Jean-Paul Sartre wrote:

> Un des traits les plus singuliers de notre époque littéraire, c'est l'apparition çà et là d'oeuvres vivaces et toutes négatives qu'on pourrait nommer des anti-romans. [...] Les anti-romans conservent l'apparence et les contours du roman; ce sont des ouvrages d'imagination qui nous présentent des personnages fictifs et nous racontent leur histoire. Mais c'est pour mieux décevoir: il s'agit de contester le roman par lui-même, de le détruire sous nos yeux dans le temps qu'on semble l'édifier, d'écrire le roman d'un roman qui ne se fait pas [...] Ces oeuvres étranges et difficilement classables ne témoignent pas de la faiblesse du genre romanesque, elles marquent seulement que nous vivons à une époque de réflexion et que le roman est en train de réfléchir sur lui-même.

These comments, general though they are, afford us an entry into an area of study, with regard to *Les Gommes*, which is of the greatest importance. Whether or not it is an 'anti-novel' (a phrase used rather casually by Sartre, raising a host of questions to which he does not address himself), *Les Gommes* is clearly a work which examines the process of writing a novel. It contains within itself a detective story and a version of the Oedipus legend, to be sure, but in addition — and perhaps more importantly — it contains a commentary on literary creation. It is a commentary on two levels: first, its very structure, style, content and tone are striking enough in themselves to constitute a demonstration of new possibilities for the novel, distinct from what is 'traditional'; second, scattered among its pages are observations and images which are designed to warn the reader, often very obliquely, that he must be prepared for something other than that which he might expect. What is intriguing is that the novel, in the words of Sartre, is being challenged through itself. Here is no direct tract against the novel as it has been accepted for years, but a work of subtle subversion. The usefulness of the framework of detective story and myth is clearly demonstrated, for the starting-point is familiar; the reader, to begin with at least, is on firm ground, guided by convention and a knowledge of what is usual, but increasingly the ground will become less firm, and *Les Gommes* will not be the novel it had seemed to be. Robbe-Grillet exploits the duality between what is expected and what is discovered; he seems constantly to be writing the former, but the reader finds himself in the latter. In this way *Les Gommes* is an excellent example of 'the novel of a novel which is not being written'.

The more accustomed one becomes to the tone and style of Robbe-Grillet's prose, the easier one finds it to identify moments when the novelist pauses to reflect on his art. Such moments may come at any time and in any situation, and the reflections may be expressed in terms which have no apparent relevance to art. They are usually brief, wry and dismissive, and the keynote is one of irony and expectation denied. Things are not what they seem, not what they 'should be', or they might be about to take an unforeseen turn.

The most obvious example is perhaps that of Wallas walking through the city. On page 52 the image is that of the detective moving purposefully forward; the elements in his progress are precisely measurable. They form a harmonious whole and are consequently reassuring:

> ... il marche et il enroule au fur et à mesure la ligne ininter-
> rompue de son propre passage, non pas une succession
> d'images déraisonnables et sans rapport entre elles, mais
> un ruban uni où chaque élément se place aussitôt dans la
> trame, même les plus fortuits, même ceux qui peuvent
> d'abord paraître absurdes, ou menaçants, ou anachroni-
> ques, ou trompeurs; ils viennent tous se ranger sagement
> l'un près de l'autre, et le tissu s'allonge sans un trou ni une
> surcharge, à la vitesse régulière de son pas. (p.52)

Wallas can be comforted because his walking gives him the feeling that he is progressing towards an end, the solution of the mystery; after an interruption provided by a confusing and ambivalent conversation he moves forward again: 'le déroulement rassurant s'est rétabli' (p.56). The detective's comfort can be shared by the reader: at moments like these, when Wallas is engaged upon the sort of business a detective habitually deals in, the novel takes on a reassuring look: the 'ruban uni' of the narrative reasserts itself, and the reader does not have to face 'une succession d'images déraisonnables et sans rapport entre elles'. Everything, however absurd, menacing, anachronistic or misleading, is in its proper place. But that 'succession d'images déraisonnables' (to which more than one unsympathetic critic has alluded) is not indefinitely postponed: Wallas's walking is not as successful as he might hope: it does not bring him to the desired goal, and there is no 'avenir inévitable et parfait' (p.52). He constantly returns, despite himself, to the Boulevard Circulaire; the 'ruban uni' is an illusion for him, and in the novel the 'ruban uni' of ordered narrative is what the reader will not find.

Immediately following this passage comes another (pp.52-53) depicting an old man reading political posters on a school wall. There are in fact three copies of the same text, an image of a clear message confidently repeated. Robbe-Grillet states, however: 'Au milieu des mots habituels se dresse çà et là comme un fanal quelque terme suspect, et la phrase qu'il éclaire de façon si louche semble un instant cacher beaucoup de choses, ou rien du tout' (p.53). In the middle of what is familiar some strange new terms stand out, perhaps full of meaning, perhaps signifying nothing. The accepted order is challenged by the unusual; the old creation is being undermined. Wallas at this point takes on momentarily the perspective of the reader, who should be warned that there will be a conflict between the coherence of the traditional novel and a certain flexibility of the new: 'Wallas reste le témoin très attentif d'un spectacle qui n'a rien perdu de ses qualités d'ordre et de permanence; peut-être au contraire la ligne devient-elle plus stricte, abandonnant peu à peu ses ornements et ses mollesses. Mais peut-être aussi cette précision d'épure n'est-elle qu'illusoire...' (p.57). The doubt of Wallas is an ironic counterpart to that of the reader who is perhaps in the grip of uncertainty as to the novel's development.

Two other series of images help Robbe-Grillet to comment upon the novel: the theatre and the mechanism of the bridge. The novel opens with the 'trois coups de torchon' of the café proprietor, signalling the beginning of the drama, and on the first page 'Quand tout est prêt, la lumière s'allume...' (p.11). Further references to scenes, decor and actors' lines, illustrating order and predictability as well as illusion, recur many times, but there is one example of particular importance: on page 23 the actor is seen suddenly to stop in the middle of a sentence, refusing to continue in the part he knows perfectly well. For a moment the play is in danger of collapse, but the actor does continue and the momentary hesitation is forgotten. Are we to see here a comment by the author, a warning that one evening the play might not run its foreseen course? The idea is seemingly dismissed, because the actor does continue, but the warning has been uttered. On page 23 Robbe-Grillet writes: 'La machinerie, parfaitement réglée, ne peut réserver la moindre surprise. Il ne s'agit que de suivre le texte, en récitant phrase après phrase, et la parole s'accomplira et Lazare sortira de sa tombe, tout enveloppé de bandelettes...'. 'La machinerie' is an echo of the bridge's mechanism, which operates in a measurable manner. It is a convenient symbol for what is well regulated and purposeful, but it is not perfect: 'par suite d'une certaine élasticité de la masse, la descente du tablier n'avait pas pris fin avec l'arrêt du mécanisme; elle s'était poursuivie pendant quelques secondes, sur un centimètre peut-être, créant un léger décalage' which suggests a more serious breakdown: 'De l'autre côté du canal, l'énorme machinerie du pont-bascule ronronne régulièrement. Il suffirait d'introduire un objet dur — qui pourrait être de dimensions très réduites — dans un engrenage essentiel et tout le système s'arrêterait, avec un grincement de mécanique détraquée' (p.220). How easy it would be to destory the mechanism of the bridge, to destroy the 'mechanism' of the novel. It is not, in effect, a question of destruction, but of reassembly: the debris in the canal (p.26) can be reassembled (p.37) in many different ways. In the place of one clearly described reality there can be perhaps 'l'espace, la tentation, la consolation du possible' (p.19). Here, Robbe-Grillet adds a wry comment: 'Comme on a la tête solide, la tentation suffit: le possible reste simplement possible, les sirènes depuis longtemps appellent sans espoir'. The new novelist may still cry in vain for some time to come...

In much the same vein, comments on Fabius become comments on the author: 'on disait déjà qu'il se méfiait des solutions simples, on chuchote maintenant qu'il a cessé de croire à l'existence d'une solution quelconque' (p.61). The notice dealing with changes in Post Office organisation suggests changes in the novel: 'Pour un profane la nature exacte de ces modifications n'apparaît pas clairement, si bien que Wallas en vient à se demander s'il y a vraiment une différence entre le nouvel état de choses et ce qui existait auparavant' (p.159), and Mme Jean's experiences at the Post Office are seen as mysterious as those described in the novel (p.192). Just as the city is dark, so *Les Gommes* is bathed in 'une clarté douteuse et fragmentaire — coupée de trous, plus ou moins largement frangés de zones de passage, où l'esprit hésite à s'aventurer' (p.121), and lest we overlook the significance of the stopping of Wallas's watch, the poster reminds us that chronology has no place here: 'Ne partez pas sans emporter *Le Temps*' (p.212).

Such examples as these do not of course add up to very much in the way of literary theory. They do not contribute particularly effectively to any undermining of the novel. They represent a series of pinpricks in the complacency and conservatism of the reader (as they appear to the author) and, often humorous and even mischievous as they are, they seem a little self-indulgent. They are designed to edge the reader further along the desired road and to provide a number of indications of what the novelist is seeking to achieve and where the desired road is leading.

It is in the structure and style of *Les Gommes* itself that the work of reflection on the novel is undertaken. The book is above all a challenge to the traditional novel's basis of coherence; in *Les Gommes* the distinction between real and unreal, true and false is blurred. Chronology is contested, and the relationships between elements are on shifting ground, because there is no ordering intelligence to do the work. There is apparently a narrator's voice distinct from the voices of the characters, but the narrator remains an observer of the present scene; he gives possibilities, not facts, and his perception is placed on the same level as that of the other characters. The reader is faced not with something which is retold, a story which is complete and finalised, he is witnessing events and perceptions as they are experienced.

In his essay 'Sur quelques notions périmées', published in 1957, Robbe-Grillet clearly identifies the specific area within fictional tradition which he is contesting:

> Tous les éléments techniques du récit — emploi systématique du passé simple et de la troisième personne, adoption sans condition du déroulement chronologique, intrigues linéaires, courbe régulière des passions, tension de chaque épisode vers une fin etc. — tout visait à imposer l'image d'un univers stable, cohérent, continu, univoque, entièrement déchiffrable. (*1*, p.31)

He criticises the manner in which traditional 'realist' authors, especially those of the nineteenth century, not only emphasise a close relationship between themselves and the world by explaining the world in terms of themselves — by making the world a reflection of their own sensibilities — but have also imposed a meaning and an order upon human experience. Balzac's fiction offers a false realism, since the point of view from which it is expressed, that of the omniscient narrator, corresponds to no possible human view, and it collates the data into a pattern of formal completeness, order and significance which makes of the reader a passive receiver of information, imposed upon him in the assumption that he will respond as every other reader responds. His creative imagination is given no scope; his individuality and his own perceptions are called into question.

In *Les Gommes* Robbe-Grillet challenges the traditional novel by removing the all-seeing eye and questioning the nature of reality. He creates a novel based not on 'what really happens' (a coherent, systematic narrative), but on characters' perceptions, including not only immediate events, but memories, fantasies, projections into the future and so on. We are in a world not of clock-time, but of human time: the forward impetus of the novel (which runs from 6 a.m. one morning to 6 a.m. the next, a cycle which, as Morrissette has shown, overlaps the other twenty-four hour cycle from 7.30 p.m. to 7.30 p.m.) is compromised by the characters' mental states, which are outside time and which, rather than merely experiencing reality, create it. The more the reader tries to reduce *Les Gommes* to its 'plot', the more he realises that he is retreating from what the novel really is, an investigation into the nature of perception and an enquiry into the process of literary creation.

In many obvious instances, narrative coherence is undermined. Among the most striking examples are those concerned with the various versions of the murder. Alongside Garinati's failed attempt at the beginning and Wallas's inadvertently successful attempt at the end, the reader finds Dupont's suicide (in two versions, pp.141 and 172), his murder by an unidentified assassin (p.173), his murder by an adolescent (p.188) and his murder by his illegitimate son in company with a dubious associate (p.203). Each of these episodes is the creation of a character (either Wallas or Laurent), as new information brings him to see the 'facts' in a new light; each one is a rearrangement, or refinement of detail. In each case the creator of the episode is responding to a stimulus which helps to give the scene its form, and while it is true that the last version of the crime which the novel contains — the murder of Dupont by Wallas — negates the others in terms of the 'plot', they are all given equal authority in terms of the novel's overall structure. No omniscient narrator evaluates them and classifies them; they are not labelled 'true' or 'false'. Dupont meets his death some seven times, and parallel to this runs the series of scenes concerning entrance to the murder house. Garinati enters on his mission (p.20); there is an ironic repeat (p.99) as Bona waits for his report. The terrified Marchat imagines his entrance into a house where he fears assassins are lying in wait (p.149), and Wallas enters to confront the killer (p.243). Dupont also enters his house, not once, but several times: to collect his papers (p.248) and earlier, returning from his classes to join his wife (in a scene Wallas is quick to banish from his mind, p.186), and to confront two killers (pp.188 and 203).

Reality is constantly changing, called into question by these repetitions and variations, which are the very antithesis of coherence and continuity. Very quickly the reader's eye, or ear, becomes accustomed to the recurring images and phrases which interlock diverse elements of the novel in a relationship which is neither temporal nor spatial. Entrances to the house are habitually accompanied by a particular phrase, or variant of it: 'Comme à l'ordinaire, la grande maison est silencieuse' (e.g. pp.141, 157, 243, 249); in a café men overheard by Wallas use phrases occuring elsewhere in the novel (p.162); the girl from the Post Office does the same (p.167). The scene on the bridge on page 157 is a variant of the scene on page 57, and there is a similar double treatment of one image on pages 181 and 221.

This list is not, of course, exhaustive, but there is enough to suggest that the reader is in the presence of a novel which is moving away from the traditional representation, or referential role, towards a new identity as a construct, as a creation which is to be examined in its own terms. The changes in register between real and imaginary, the juxtaposition of individual perceptions of reality, the repetitions and variations of phrases and images are not so many stylistic devices used to throw light on a central core of meaning within the novel; they become the end in themselves, the patterning of the prose with its own rhythms and structures.

The process of *Les Gommes* is far from complete, and the nature of this particular novel as experimental must be emphasised. Robbe-Grillet has certainly not abandoned the anecdote, and his characters are clearly men and women whose behaviour is susceptible of a degree of psychological interpretation. The world of *Les Gommes* is familiar, with its streets, shops, trams and railway-station; the people in it have preoccupations which are easily recognisable. That core of familiarity is essential to Robbe-Grillet, who is well aware that his reader is steeped in a tradition of realist prose fiction, and that he is accustomed to relating the phenomena within the novel to a world outside it. He thus plays a double game: he represents that world in a form, the detective story, which emphasises still further the familiarity, and subverts it by imposing upon it other patterns, be they that of schematic images and phrases, be they that of the Oedipus legend, which set up a whole network of resonances of their own, and become not *meaning*, but *form*.

In effect *Les Gommes* is a demonstration, albeit in an incomplete way, of Robbe-Grillet's refusal to distinguish between 'form' and 'content'. He expresses the view in 'Sur quelques notions périmées' that nothing is more absurd than the typical phrase beloved of critics, 'Un tel a quelque chose à dire et il le dit bien'. The true author has nothing to say, merely a way to speaking. This is not to say that his art is gratuitous or without meaning: it has, if it is successful, a necessity, but it is an inner one, a necessity which is not defined in terms of usefulness or relevance to anything outside itself. Robbe-Grillet is well aware of the problem: '... l'oeuvre doit s'imposer comme nécessaire, mais nécessaire *pour rien*; son architecture est sans emploi; sa force est une force inutile' (*1*, p.43).

If *Les Gommes* is approached in this way, a new level of significance appears, one of structure and internal patterning. The reader has to become aware of theme and variation, leitmotif, repetition, juxtaposition, combination, image and variant. As J.-L. Seylaz puts it, in such a reading, 'Au suspens dramatique traditionnel: que va faire tel ou tel personnage de fiction, s'est substitué le suspens scriptural: que va produire tel mot, comment va se transformer telle séquence' (*18*, p.125). Robbe-Grillet allows that such 'formalism' is accepted in music, but meets with reluctance in the world of the novel, and indeed it does require from the reader not only good-will, in forsaking well nourished expectations, but great attentiveness: nothing is more taxing than the reading of a novel with one eye (or rather, both eyes) on its technique. Moreover, the reader may well sense an ambivalence in his position: is he free to create the internal patterning in his own way, or is he required to identify a scheme imposed by the author? The author may well have nothing to say, but what is the extent of his editorial authority when it comes to his way of speaking? There may be no omniscient narrator, but is there not, nonetheless, the author behind his text, exercising his prerogative of selection and design?

Les Gommes, it seems, offers the reader a wide scope. The images and themes which dominate the book are imposed by the author through the narrative structure: the demands of the detective story and the Oedipus myth provide him with his primary material, which is further shaped by the perception of the characters. Key elements are thus chosen, for example, the murder house, the streets of the city, the erasers, and they are enclosed in a seemingly circular structure (the epilogue contains similar elements to those found in the prologue, and Wallas at the end is back where he started). Within that structure the reader is free to a remarkable extent, not only in terms of interpreting the significance of the Oedipus myth (as we have said, it is not possible to make a simple identification between Wallas and Oedipus, because Robbe-Grillet has deliberately not given enough information), but also in terms of 'reconstructing' the text. The particular quality of Robbe-Grillet pictures (the murder house, the mechanism of the bridge, the Greek temple) is an immediacy, conveyed by a precision of terminology, but one devoid of depth. Since he consciously limits himself to surface descriptions, the immediacy contains within it a void; the author's voice stops short at the moment the reader expects him to continue, and so it is the reader who continues. Faced with multiple versions of a similar scene, or striking juxtapositions (for example, the series of scenes on pages 112-121 concerning the man in the raincoat at Dupont's gate), the reader adds his own voice: he is responding to pictures, not to meanings.

The reader may well at times be clearly pushed in a certain direction: as B. Morrissette has shown (*13*, p.58), references to the staircase in Dupont's house, with its 'vingt et une marches de bois, plus, tout en bas, une marche de pierre blanche' (p.24) may be drawn from the Tarot pack of cards, with its twenty-two 'arcanes majeures' — twenty-one numbered cards and one without a number. This last card is the Fou du Roi, and on the bottom stair stands '... une colonne de cuivre aux ornementations compliquées, terminée en guise de pomme par une tête de fou coiffé du bonnet à trois clochettes' (p.24). The sixteenth card of the series is La Maison Dieu, with its significance of unexpected happening and downfall, and on four occasions (pp.24, 40, 150 and 243), reference is made to the painting which hangs over the sixteenth stair. Here, as with the Oedipus myth, Robbe-Grillet is presenting a possible line of approach, another way of arranging

the elements within the novel. But no precise identification between painting and meaning is possible. The reader can take as
little or as much from the descriptions as he chooses.

We thus have an intriguing conjunction of forces within the
novel, which is built up on different levels, not all of which are
totally compatible. It shows particularly Robbe-Grillet's desire
to break the bond which he sees uniting traditional realist fiction
with a world of order and meaning. He is anxious to look with a
new eye at the relationship between man and the world — a
world which for him has no significance beyond the bare fact of
its existence — and to examine equally critically the foundations
on which prose fiction rests. The time-honoured techniques
must be called into question; the novel must progress beyond its
accepted role as reality's counterfeiter. Here, of course, further
difficulties begin: how far is it possible to dispense with
character and plot and write a novel, as it were from nothing and
about nothing? How far can one combat the reader's ingrained
liking for literary realism? Is it possible to dissociate language
from its roots in the 'real' world? *Les Gommes* asks the questions rather than providing the answer. It undermines the importance of plot and offers no character analysis, yet it deals
throughout its length with the significance of actions and with
men and women who move in a recognisable world and impose
their meaning on it. As the previous section of this study sought
to show, the novel has a strikingly visual character, emphasising
that man is here among objects, things of this world. *Les
Gommes* is far from being a complete statement on these matters, and the paradoxes and tensions which are apparent, particularly those between the referential and the non-referential,
are not altogether satisfactorily resolved.

5. *Le Voyeur:* The Outer Reality — Mathias the Watch-Salesman

Le Voyeur, like *Les Gommes*, has something of the detective story, or mystery thriller, about it. The centrepiece of this, Robbe-Grillet's second published novel, is a crime, and the novel's structure is dictated by the anticipation of that crime and the reactions to it once it has been committed. The reader is a witness to the pressures upon the principal character, Mathias, which apparently lead him to an act of violence, and his subsequent attempts to avoid detection and construct a plausible alibi. The reader, in effect, is placed in the role of the detective — for there is no such figure in this novel — and is faced with the task of interpreting information and making out of it a significant whole. The task is in many respects a difficult one, made deliberately so by the author's refusal, as in his earlier novel, to provide an explanation of the different elements in the book. There is a framework of action which can be retrieved from *Le Voyeur*, but it can be done only in somewhat indistinct terms. There are certain events, characters and places, but at the same time there is a great deal of uncertainty as to what has happened, why and in what way it has happened.

This uncertainty is the result primarily of a striking narrative device: the crime itself is not described. There is a blank page, at the end of the first part, which represents the central 'event' of the novel. There is a void around which everything is organised, and the reader reads in the first part a preparation for and in the remainder of the book a response to a crime which he has to piece together from scattered items of information. The crime is, then, in a very real sense, absent: amid the clues provided by Mathias's vision, clearly that of a sexual obsessive, and by his anxious attempts to 'rearrange' events so that he cannot be suspected, there remains a central hole in the narrative. Did the crime really take place, or is it imagined? Is Mathias guilty of indecent assault and murder, or is he merely a man given to sexual fantasies? The absence of a fixed point of reference — a description of the act in question — indicates that Robbe-Grillet's interests are other than those of merely telling a story or presenting a dramatic case-history; it indicates also that the answers to the questions posed above will not be readily forthcoming and that the questions themselves are perhaps not the right ones. As before, Robbe-Grillet is raising questions about the nature and the function of the novel itself and hopes to lead the reader to view *Le Voyeur* not as a puzzle ingeniously presented, containing one acceptable solution, but as an enquiry into the capabilities, limits and methods of prose fiction. As with *Les Gommes*, the plot is not dispensed with, but it does not have the characteristics of a well-ordered sequence of past events 'objectively' described. In the novel there is a double perspective: there is the voice of a narrator, who describes the actions of Mathias, and there is also the voice of Mathias himself. The narrator's view is interrupted and distorted by the perspective of Mathias, with his dreams, memories and fantasies. 'Normal' time, causality and sequence are constantly coming up against Mathias's inner world. Once again, Robbe-Grillet is undermining the traditional supports of the novel and making the reader work hard to pick up the clues: the reader has to be very attentive if he is to be in a position to interpret Mathias's actions and character.

Interpretations (as we shall see in the next chapter of this study) have not been lacking, and reactions to the novel have been predictably varied. J. Mistler considers the novel to be completely arbitrary (*10*, p.23), whereas B.F. Stoltzfus finds a 'deterministic pattern of things and events' (*20*, p.501). M. Blanchot considers the novel to be without a centre (because the crime is not described) (*10*, p.28), while Colette Audry, accepting the centre to be murder, deduces it only from the second and third parts (*3*, p.262). She describes the gaze which Mathias directs upon the objects about him as 'le regard déhumanisé, déstabilisé, objectal en un mot, d'une simple lentille de verre, d'un pur objectif' (*3*, p.267), thus placing herself in the tradition of Barthes and his 'primauté du regard', whereas Hazel E. Barnes (*4*) and B. Morrissette (*13*), like Stoltzfus, see the novel in

terms of its subjectivity. The variety of these responses is an indication of the novel's complexity and the tension created by the
double perspective referred to above: the only information
offered to the reader concerning the murder of Jacqueline Leduc
is provided by the consciousness of Mathias. That consciousness
deforms rather than relates events, and the pathological distortion it brings succeeds only in masking from the reader any
'truth' he might reasonably expect. The voice of the narrator is
limited to external descriptions, and tantalisingly stops short of
imposing any corrective upon the subjective view of Mathias;
thus 'truth, or 'what really happened', is constantly avoided,
and left to the imagination of the reader.

It is nonetheless possible to retrieve a framework within which
the action of the novel takes place, and to set out what the reader
may safely deduce from the narration. Mathias, a travelling
watch-salesman, returns to his native island, three hours' ferry
journey from the mainland, to go on a sales trip for one day.
The novel at once offers a clearly defined context in terms of
space and time. This island is described if not minutely at least
carefully, and with some precision; the reader follows Mathias
on his visit to the village which surrounds the port, where the
arrangement of the streets, houses and cafés is noted, and
further afield to the hamlets which lie around the island. The
dimensions of the island are recorded, as well as the nature and
disposition of its major features. Details of the customs,
attitudes and dress of the inhabitants are introduced to provide a
convincing background to the drama. Such details are not introduced gratuitously; there is no attempt by the author to provide
a complete picture. Instead, everything is communicated
through the experience of Mathias, be it in terms of his
childhood memories, through information which he gathers
before his departure from the mainland, or through his observations as he journeys across the island.

Indeed there is a certain ambivalence at work. Careful attention is paid to the vegetation and to the topography, as well as to
the means of livelihood of those who live there; all this, and, in
addition, observations on language and proper names, has led
one critic, Erwin Rault, to suggest that a 'model' for the island

could be found in Brittany (*15*, p.26). He is, however, quick to point out that the validity of such a supposition is weakened by the use of the 'couronne' (a 'northern' coin) as the unit of currency, and, more importantly, by the way in which the island has no existence independent of Mathias's experience of it. Its function is not that of a geographical entity which Mathias comes to visit, but rather that of the place where his personal drama unfolds; the island exists only in terms of Mathias's perception of it and as the setting for his particular crisis. It would be possible, as Rault points out, to draw a plan of the island from information scattered among the pages of the novel; the fact that it is so scattered, and introduced only in relation to Mathias, indicates that such a plan would run counter to the author's intentions.

If the spatial dimensions of *Le Voyeur* are less than clearly defined, despite the amount of detail given, the same is true of its temporal dimensions. Time is constantly mentioned, and much of the drama is played out against an awareness of passing time. Mathias arrives on the island conscious that he has only a limited period at his disposal: he lands on Tuesday at 10 a.m. in the morning, and is due to leave again at 4.15 that afternoon. He has before him six and a quarter hours, and in order to ensure that he uses them to his best advantage, he undertakes calculations concerning the maximum number of minutes he can devote to any one sale (p.34). These calculations are repeated in revised form as circumstances change (pp.52, 81). With recent business having been slack, and with Mathias haunted by the fear that he might have to change his job once again (p.27), estimates of how time is to be spent, complemented by calculations over his likely income, reflect his anxiety and his desire to succeed.

It is possible to recover from the text much of the chronology of the day, but it is notable that such a chronology is not given particular emphasis in the novel and is not Robbe-Grillet's prime concern. Clock-time, running from 10 a.m. to 4.15 p.m., is challenged and undermined by two other factors; firstly by Mathias's 'inner' time, his perception which exists in a timescale of its own, and secondly by his need to rearrange events and provide his own account of them. The first of these factors is properly the subject of the next chapter of this study; it is

however appropriate at this stage to point out that the novel's
forward movement, imparted by the passage of clock-time and
the steady approach of the time limit of the ferry's departure, is
counterbalanced by the distortions effected by Mathias's own
vision. We are given, at different moments, direct access to the
mind of a man under various degrees of stress, a mind which,
because of its particular characteristics, constantly returns to his
childhood and to more immediate past events, and which is also
given to fantasies and projections into the future.

The second factor which challenges and undermines clock-
time gives the novel its particular tone of suspense. In the second
and third parts Mathias is concerned to manufacture a timetable
of his movements which will render him above suspicion, and
which will entail the accounting for a missing hour, the hour
when the crime takes place. The early part of his day, if it does
not go according to plan, is at least unexceptional and relatively
uncomplicated. After landing at 10 a.m. Mathias goes to the
café to hire a bicycle, but is told that he must wait three-quarters
of an hour (p.49). He spends that time visiting the immediate
neighbourhood (the triangular square, the shops, various apart-
ments and houses) in an attempt to do some business; his efforts
are not successful, and he rests by sitting on the rocky shore near
the jetty. It is here that he realises it is 11.05 (p.78). He is already
aware that he has wasted too much time: when he left the café
(p.69) he had felt the need to hurry on: 'Mais il n'avait déjà que
trop perdu de temps et il ne s'attarda pas à se chauffer au soleil',
and now, at last provided with his bicycle, he is anxious to catch
up with his projected programme (p.81). He stops at the last
house in the village and visits Mme Leduc, whose brother he has
already met on the mainland (p.32). It is here that he sees the
photograph of her youngest daughter, Jacqueline, and discovers
her likely whereabouts. After this visit he tries to make even
quicker progress, although the reader (as will be shown in the
next chapter) is aware that he is not driven on solely by business
concerns. He stops at two further isolated houses, but his haste
is so great that he fails to conclude likely sales. When he reaches
the crossroads, where one path leads to the cliff, where
Jacqueline is guarding sheep (p.87), it is 11.30.

The first part ends with Mathias following that path, and the second part begins with him on the main road again. Now he is conscious of the oddity of his position at this moment, dismounted from his bicycle and contemplating the body of a dead frog, particularly when he realises that he has been seen by the approaching Mme Marek, and immediately the reader is aware that Mathias is feeling some kind of guilt. The pages which follow offer a striking demonstration of Robbe-Grillet's skill in conveying that guilt without naming it or analysing it. At first, Mathias briefly speculates as to whether Mme Marek could have seen from which direction he had come (p.92); then he feels the need to explain his halt by examining his machine for mechanical failure (pp.92-3). He prepares one account of his actions (pp.93-4) which differs in two respects from details given in the first part. When he engages in conversation with Mme Marek, he gives another version (p.96) which includes a visit to the Marek farm. This account is repeated in amplified form (pp.97-101).

For the moment the reader has no indication of the time, and it will not be until nearly twenty pages later (on p.118) that he will be told that when, for the first time since leaving the village, Mathias looks at his watch, it is 1.07 p.m. By then, further evidence will have been provided to lend weight to the reader's suspicions that there is a gap, that something has gone unrecorded. Mathias's behaviour is dominated by a growing concern with the immediate past: he gives another account of his movements to the *patronne* of the café at the hamlet of Les Roches Noires in which he again claims to have visited the Marek farm, but he seems to sense a danger in doing so: 'Il valait mieux s'arrêter. Ces précisions de temps et d'itinéraires — fournies et demandées — étaient inutiles, suspectes même, pis encore: confuses' (p.114). He uses the words 'alibis' (p.114) and 'truquage' (p.115), and seems above all concerned to assure himself that he was not seen at any time in a place outside his supposed itinerary; this seems particularly important to him because of the news that Jacqueline Leduc has disappeared and Maria, her elder sister, has been looking for her, has visited the café and mentioned the watch-salesman. Mathias attempts to

account for Maria's movements and to relate the respective
itineraries of the girl and himself. He is plunged into a world of
hypothesis and speculation, and constantly obliged to reassess
his understanding of the significance of Maria's actions and the
plausibility of his own version of his day. He fears that he will
have to start all over again (pp.109, 113), and cannot stop
himself returning to the question. The calculations of the earlier
part, before Mathias set out, have been replaced by different
calculations which, the reader senses, are to be used to disguise
rather than reveal the truth.

What might be the 'truth' is occasionally glimpsed as Robbe-
Grillet, with great skill, evokes the mind of a man suffering considerable stress. The reader is obliged to relate disparate
elements which are presented to him without any explanation;
there is the continuing need of Mathias to settle upon a version
of his movements (pp.116, 148), but frequently there are glimp-
ses of other concerns in his mind. Following a striking passage
(p.117) where he remembers his visit to the Leduc house, and
particularly the photograph of the young girl (the word
'photographie' is used six times in two lines), Mathias is beset by
images of a scene on the clifftop (pp.122, 133). There is a
fleeting suggestion in his conversation with the *patronne* (p.119)
that he is familiar with the clifftop, and he puts forward the idea
that the missing girl might have fallen at a dangerous spot. In
later pages the images of a confrontation between a girl and a
traveller become sharper, but they are seen in terms not of Jacqueline but of Violette, a name used earlier (pp.83, 84) in scenes
of a more clearly erotic nature. When Mathias goes to the home
of Jean Robin and the conversation turns to Jacqueline, Mathias
lets slip 'une parole maladroite': 'Elle ne viendra plus
maintenant' (p.142), a remark which is one of the clearest indications that he is seeking to suppress information rather than
to elucidate it, and that the uncertainty he feels and the confusion in his mind (p.143) are the result of a deep and troubling
anxiety.

As Mathias resumes his itinerary after his lunch with Jean
Robin, the chronology of the narrative is reaffirmed, as the need
for sales becomes imperative. Mathias is once again aware of the

passage of time, and as he pedals his way across the island he looks more frequently at his watch: 3.30, p.156; 3.50, p.157; 4.05, p.158. The vigour he displays in his sales attempts and his pedalling would seem to indicate the extent of his anxiety. Because of the mechanical failure of the bicycle (an irony here, as he has earlier 'invented' one to account for his actions), he misses the ferry, and, realising that he will now be forced to spend three more days on the island, he wonders if there are any policemen there (p.162).

The third part of the novel reinforces the sense of Mathias's guilt. It begins with a reminder, with the use of the cinema poster and the title, 'Monsieur X. sur le double circuit' (p.167), that much of Mathias's energy has been directed towards the establishment of an alternative arrangement of events. Now, with the discovery of Jacqueline's body at the foot of the cliffs (p.174), his actions are apparently directed towards the recovery of any material which might incriminate him, in particular the remains of three cigarettes which, the reader can guess, have been used to torture the victim. His search leads him to a dramatic confrontation with the young companion of Jean Robin; she suspects Jean (p.183), and produces one of the cigarettes as proof, as well as ascribing Mathias's 'parole maladroite' to Jean. Her friendship with the dead girl is, however, potentially dangerous to Mathias, because she can establish reasonably precisely the time when the murder took place. Mathias is put into much greater danger by the behaviour of the young Julien Marek, who, when Mathias finally visits the farm, confirms the false account of an earlier, imaginary visit. Again, as at the beginning of the second part of the novel, Robbe-Grillet's presentation of his material is particularly skilful. He has to show Mathias's anxious reaction to the boy's lies and his feverish attempts to find reasons for them (pp.200 sqq). Mathias has to go back over the day's events once more, this time in order to accommodate Julien Marek in them, for he is aware of the insufficiency of the version he has settled on: 'Après s'être tellement acharné à la confection de cet alibi — comme s'il eût été de nature à le laver de tout soupçon — Mathias s'apercevait à présent de son insuffisance. Le séjour sur la falaise avait duré trop longtemps pour qu'on pût le résorber tout entier de cette manière. Un trou demeurait toujours dans l'emploi du temps' (p.201). The need to find the remaining missing cigarette is more urgent, and while searching for it Mathias meets Julien, who, it becomes apparent, is not only a witness to Mathias's attempts to dispose of the incriminating overcoat (p.205), but has also found a piece of string, the third cigarette and a sweet-wrapper of the same kind as those covering sweets which Mathias bought earlier. Not only this: Julien was probably a witness to the crime itself. Mathias's confusion is increased by the unrelenting stare and uncommunicativeness of the boy; he is forced in his mind to go over his actions in order to find explanations which he knows to be unconvincing. The boy does not pursue his interrogation, but Mathias has been severely shocked, and a little later loses consciousness in the café at Les Roches Noires (p.222).

This crisis passes; although Mathias momentarily fears that he is being sought by the police (p.238), he regains sufficient composure to refuse the offer of a crossing to the mainland in a fishing-boat (p.241), and seems no longer in a hurry to leave the island, wishing perhaps to assure himself that he has adequately covered his tracks. He disposes of potentially incriminating material, such as cigarettes, sweets and a newspaper cutting, and it is as if the crime gradually recedes from his mind, a process symbolised perhaps by the work of *nettoyage* undertaken in the harbour (p.240) and the blank cinema poster (p.250). He can, after all, enjoy the irony of the fact that he alone on the island had no reason to dislike Jacqueline or to hold a grudge against her (p.185), and he leaves unhindered on the Friday afternoon ferry.

So much, then, is recoverable, and yet the reader is made increasingly aware that the clearer this context becomes, the further away he draws from what *Le Voyeur* essentially is. The 'plot', as before, has lost its quality of certainty: seen in terms of significant events, limited in time and space and organised into an ordered sequence, it is not at the heart of the novel, waiting to be identified and accepted. Rather, it is part of a greater whole, a network of elements, psychological, literary and structural, which make *Le Voyeur* a more complex work of art than a mystery thriller.

6. *Le Voyeur:* The Inner Reality — Mathias the Psychopath

While *Le Voyeur* can be read as the story of a watch-salesman's activities on a brief visit to his native island, it can also be read as a powerful representation of a psychic disorder, and it is on the 'inner reality' of Mathias that considerable critical attention has been focussed. Interpretations of Mathias in psychological and medical terms have not been lacking. Rault describes Mathias as 'un obsédé sexuel' and adduces further evidence of schizophrenia (*15*, p.51), an interpretation Morrissette repeats, with some amplification. He sees Mathias as 'un cas classique de schizophrénie cyclique, teintée d'érotomanie sadique' (*13*, p.103). Stoltzfus sees Mathias as 'the victim of a compulsive behaviour pattern' and speaks of his 'psychosexual infantilism' (*20*, p.501), while R. Weil-Malherbe goes further into medical analysis, describing Mathias as 'un cas d'épilepsie du type psychomoteur' (*22*). Amid such riches Jean Alter sounds a quiet note of scepticism: 'Le livre terminé, on ne sera guère plus avancé dans la connaissance de ses ressorts psychologiques. Le nombre d'explications proposées par les critiques témoigne de la nature insaisissable de son caractère et, partant, des raisons de son acte' (*2*, p.27).

Alter's comment can indeed be seen as a warning to the reader of the difficulties facing him in his attempts to come to terms with a character who remains ultimately elusive. Robbe-Grillet, as in *Les Gommes*, has rejected any notion of psychological analysis, and has preferred to translate Mathias's mental processes into pictures. These constantly intrude upon the third-person narration in the novel, introducing a note of confusion and deformation into descriptions of the material world. Once again, what the eye sees will define the seer, and the reader will have to learn to decode the particular selectivity which Mathias operates, and decide whether it bears witness, as Stoltzfus suggests, to 'a deterministic pattern of things and events from which he cannot extricate himself' (*20*, p.501).

A particular difficulty is, of course, provided by the fact that the crime itself is not described. Is Mathias suffering from amnesia, is he imagining a crime, which, for whatever reason, is attractive to him, or is he seeking to repress the thought of it? Mathias's approach to the crime is oblique in that, unable or unwilling to contemplate it as a single continuous event, he comes to it piece by piece, firstly in anticipation, as it takes shape in his mind out of the stimuli he encounters in the first part of the novel, and secondly in retrospect, as particular elements of it are brought to his mind. The pattern of the crime is constantly changing; different images are offered on different occasions, and in the absence of anything remotely resembling a 'definitive version' the reader is unable to decide what actually took place and whether, at any given moment, Mathias is being factual or hallucinating. Indeed, here lies the whole point of the exercise: there is no 'real' crime which the reader can identify, only Mathias's perception of it, disorganised and erratic though that perception may be. Robbe-Grillet is inviting the reader to speculate not upon the crime itself but upon the significance of the crime for Mathias. In that sense, the guilt or innocence of Mathias is irrelevant; what should be considered is what light the images associated with the crime throw upon him. Jean Alter may well be right in asserting that the reader is likely to be persuaded that Mathias did kill the girl, for his actions and preoccupations in the second and third parts of the novel would make no sense if they were merely dictated by what Alter calls 'une imagination malade' (*2*, p.27). A feeling of guilt on the part of Mathias is clearly discernible, and adds a note of urgency to much of what he does, but it remains impossible to say whether the guilt corresponds to an action actually committed or not. The only certainties are the images which crowd in upon Mathias and constitute his 'film intérieur', and it is through the medium of these images that Robbe-Grillet can provide elements which the reader must assemble into a coherent pattern.

There are certain recurring images which, from the very beginning of the novel, suggest particular obsessions of Mathias and intimate that his view of the world is constantly deformed by those obsessions. For example, on page 10 Mathias sees on the ferry a young girl who is apparently looking in his direction; on page 22 the description of the girl is amplified, and now she is leaning against an iron pillar, with her hands behind her back and her legs slightly apart. Her bearing is graceful and Mathias notes: 'Son visage reflétait la douceur à la fois confiante et réfléchie dont l'imagination pare les bonnes élèves.' The reader does not know if she is 'really' standing in that position or not: it is sufficient that Mathias sees her like that, in an attitude which, at different points in the novel, will be significantly modified. On page 29 the description is almost identical to that on page 22, with the new note, 'Ses yeux démesurément ouverts...': the first suggestion of the girl's fear and submissiveness has been introduced. On page 59 the girl in the café (who three pages earlier had been described as frightened and cowed) puts her hands behind her back, apparently to tie her apron: she does so as fishermen in the café are discussing what punishment would be appropriate for a wayward young girl, and it is then that Mathias puts his hand into his pocket to touch the piece of string which, as we shall see, takes on a particularly sinister significance. The girl on the ferry is remembered again on page 75, when she is clearly imagined as being tied to the pillar, and is transformed on page 83 and page 84 in an evocative scene. Mathias is looking at the photograph of Jacqueline Leduc but imposing upon it the image of Violette, possibly the victim of a vicious sexual crime described in the newspaper cutting which Mathias keeps in his wallet (p.76). Now Violette is tied to the trunk of a tree, and Mathias's imagination, deforming the banal snapshot, dwells upon details which suggest that physical violence is likely to ensue. In this context the name Violette has hardly been chosen at random: this form of diminutive, echoing as it does *viol* or *violer*, contributes throughout the novel further suggestions of sexual aggression, as well as that unsettling note of passivity and submission on the part of the victim.

It is almost immediately after looking at the photograph that Mathias will take the path leading to the cliffs (p.87), and Robbe-Grillet has sought to implant in the reader's mind a clear suggestion of the watch-salesman's obsessions, for the repeated view of a young girl with her hands behind her back, an image increasing in its intensity and sexual overtones, is part of a series of interrelating images of sexual violence. Among these is that on pages 28-9, when Mathias, walking through the town in the early morning to catch the ferry to the island, hears what could be a cry of distress, and sees, or imagines, a violent scene, with a man standing in a bedroom, his arm raised as if to strike another person. Features of the scene — the bed, the lamp, the packet of cigarettes, the young female victim — are repeatedly reintroduced in varying patterns in later scenes, notably in the description of the cinema poster (pp.45, 46, 80) depicting in strident colours a gigantic man in Renaissance costume holding close to him a young woman, one hand at her throat, the other hand forcibly keeping her hands locked behind her back. As he goes about the business of selling watches, while waiting for the bicycle, Mathias's imagination imposes on the world about him a series of images which run along ominously repetitive lines: a visit to an apartment (p.66) revives the earlier bedroom images, adding the character of a young girl in a nightdress saying her prayers. Mathias's attention is drawn to the nape of her neck, a detail he had noted twice (pp.58, 63) on the girl in the café. She had a frightened demeanour, and her employer, the café proprietor, resembled the figure in the cinema poster (p.61). The frightened girl, the gigantic man and various features of the bedroom reappear on pages 76-8, when Mathias reads the newspaper cutting; he is sitting on the shore, and mention is made of the waves breaking 'avec un bruit de gifle' (pp.75, 78 and earlier, p.15).

Such controlled repetition as this alerts the attentive reader: Robbe-Grillet, without once being explicit, is intent upon projecting the content of an obsessive individual consciousness. The keynote is in effect one of imminent and barely contained violence; the images are highly suggestive because they are not explicit, but contain a large measure of menace. The image of the frightened, submissive girl is echoed by the repetition of the word 'poupée' (pp.23, 46, 64, 72, 78); the interior of Mathias's samples case is decorated with small pictures of dolls, and on page 72 he specifically looks at these pictures. This preoccupation with what is at one and the same time the customary toy of a young girl and a symbol of helplessness and vulnerability is of course significant, particularly when it is developed through Mathias's awareness of the tailor's dummy in the shop (p.71), which is dressed in women's underwear and which he sees in terms of the mutilated body of a young woman. Once he has seen this, Mathias seems particularly conscious of the shopkeeper's physical appearance and 'la base fragile du cou' (p.71).

These details exploit a fairly common currency, and the sexuality implicit in these scenes is obvious. They are couched in generalised but evocative terms, propelling the reader in a particular direction without imposing specific or limiting meanings. The reader is given enough detail to begin the drawing up of a convincing portrait, but enough scope to place the emphases where he will. Robbe-Grillet provides further, more idiosyncratic elements, of which the most notable is the piece of string. Repeatedly mention is made of a particular piece of string which Mathias picks up and places in his pocket. At certain moments he puts his hand into his pocket to touch it; on pages 17 and 22 this action is followed by his looking at the other passengers on the ferry (perhaps looking for the young girl?), and on other occasions (e.g. p.59) it is associated with clearly erotic preoccupations. In the early stages of the novel the full significance of the string — that it will be used to tie the victim — obviously escapes the reader; for the moment the string is presented as an echo of childhood, for the young Mathias apparently collected pieces of string and preserved them in a cardboard box. The echo of childhood is a disquieting one, as Stoltzfus suggests: 'Numerous flashbacks reveal that Mathias's psychosexual infantilism has its origins in childhood behaviour, as for instance, the reference to bits of string used for games with algae and sea-anemones, "toutes sortes d'amusements compliqués et incertains"' (*20*, p.501), and Stoltzfus points to a common theme of Robbe-Grillet's novels: '...the behaviour patterns of Robbe-Grillet's adult protagonists have as their generative source childhood experiences' (*20*, p.502). Mathias is taken back to childhood not only by the string, but by the sight of seagulls, for in his mind rests a particular scene when as a young boy he spent a whole afternon drawing a seabird (p.18). The suggestion is clearly that Mathias the adult has not thrown off all the effects of his childhood and that his emotional development may have been hindered. Despite the fact that he intends to limit his visit to the island to purely professional concerns and not to seek out his birthplace, he will imagine a return to his younger days at the end of the novel (p.230).

If the string is to take on greater significance later in the novel, the same is true of the packet of cigarettes which Mathias buys. Cigarettes feature in some of his fantasies, which include the burning of a young girl as a witch (p.85); they will be used to torture the victim, just as the sweets he buys (immediately after contemplating the tailor's dummy) will be used to gain her confidence. The other notable obsession of Mathias is the figure 8, which recurs in many forms — as the impression left by two rings on the harbour wall, as bicycle wheels, as holes in a door, as eyes, as the shape of Mathias's itinerary and so on. As Stoltzfus puts it, 'Mathias responds to the figure 8 as Pavlov's dog to the bell' (*20*, p.503), and Stoltzfus notes the overtly sexual imagery of 'une excroissance rougeâtre qui semblait être le pivot' (p.17) and the phallic symbolism of the rusty piton.

It is, then, reasonable to say that, as he pedals urgently towards the crossroads (p.86), Mathias's state of mind and sexual obsession has been forcefully, if imprecisely suggested. The frequent use of the name Violette further indicates that he is in the grip of some pressing fantasy (or memory?) which he will need to assuage; the contrasting images on page 87 of a mounting sea, striking the shore with force, and the more gentle waves in the channel offer the visual reinforcement of the ideas of desire and satisfaction. These two states will continue to be illustrated in the second and third parts of the novel, with, of course, a different emphasis: the crime has been committed and persists in Mathias's mind as a memory. It is inextricably linked with the possibility of detection and his need to assure himself of a convincing alibi, and thus the images will take on greater or lesser degrees of intensity according to his sense of danger. There are nonetheless certain constant patterns which reinforce the reader's impression of an obsessive, even deranged personality.

The second part opens with Mathias gazing at the body of a dead frog, and seeing it in crude sexual terms. Following this, his anxiety concerning the possibility of being questioned about his itinerary because of the enquiries made by Jacqueline's sister, ensures that images associated with the crime stay in his mind. Not only is the woman behind the bar in the café at Les Roches Noires seen momentarily in the familiar terms of fear and submissiveness (p.106), but the indistinctly overheard conversation of two customers (p.108) suggests to Mathias the words 'falaise' and 'lier', a case no doubt of his adapting what is said to what is uppermost in his mind. As he reconstructs his recent timetable to account for his whereabouts, his mind returns to elements of the drama, notably to the clifftop itself, showing that Mathias is familiar with it: 'dans le creux abrité où broutaient les brebis...' (p.112). The memory of the scene in the Leduc house (p.117) contains the striking repetition of the word 'photographie' to emphasise what had earlier caught Mathias's attention. His mind is taken again to the clifftop when he hears a voice in the café say, 'Pour ça, ne craignez rien: elle est vive!' (p.120). His response, 'Vive. Elle était. Vive. Vivante. Brûlée vive', is significant because it introduces, through the past tense of the verb, not only the suggestion that Mathias knows that the girl is dead, but how she met her death.

A fleeting reference to the newspaper cutting (p.120) serves to remind the reader of Mathias's interest in a crime of violence, and when, on page 122, there is further mention of events on the clifftop, Mathias conceives of the girl as Violette, and pictures her waiting passively, looking towards him in a somewhat indeterminate fashion, in much the same way as the girl on the ferry (p.11). That earlier image will come to him later (p.161) as he watches the ferry depart, but before that Mathias will on other occasions betray his fantasies: during his visit to the home of Jean Robin he interprets the relationship between his host and the girl living with him in terms of dominant male and submissive female. His attention is drawn to the nape of her neck, but now (pp.145, 152) a note of violence is added with the reference to a scratch and drops of blood.

This last detail notwithstanding, the urgency of Mathias's sexual preoccupations gradually diminishes. In the last pages of the second part of the novel, where his attention is directed to making as many sales as possible before his hurried return to the harbour, and in the third part, where he seeks to remove incriminating evidence, images of sexual obsession become notably less frequent. When they are brought to Mathias's mind, it is in response to external stimuli. When Mathias, forced to remain on the island until Friday, is obliged to look for somewhere to stay, he is told that Mme Leduc has on occasion rented a room, and the mention of the name causes him not only to visualise elements of the scene on the clifftop, but to imagine climbing the stairs in the Leduc house and seeing the young Violette. This image ends with the dramatic repetition of Violette's name (p.171). Immediately afterwards, Mathias's mind, as he asks at the café for a room, returns to earlier bedroom scenes. When he does find accommodation in a house near the harbour, the room which he is to occupy appears to him as similar to the room he occupied as a child; he notes that the large table would be suitable not only for writing upon, but also for drawing upon (p.173) — a reference back to the scene when as a child he drew the seagull — and one of the large cupboards is identified as a possible hiding-place for a collection of pieces of string (p.174). His childhood is recalled again on pages 229-32.

In this way the reader is not allowed to forget those pressures which have been suggested earlier, but the tone is now clearly more subdued. There is repeated use of the phrase 'Mathias se passa la main sur les yeux' (e.g. pp.171, 172, 191 twice) and its variants 'Mathias se passa la main sur le front' (e.g. pp.213, 222) and '...sur le visage' (p.215), which may well suggest that while he is still concerned with the danger of discovery, he is less preoccupied with the crime itself. He is able to distance himself from it; the gesture described in these phrases suggests anxiety, but also an awareness of the crime as a crime, as behaviour deviating from the normal, and not as the means to assuage violent desires. He burns the newspaper cutting (p.236), showing perhaps that, momentarily at least, he has come to terms with his obsessions, and when the sight of the waitress's hand and wrist on the breakfast table (p.245) takes his mind back to the bound wrists of Jacqueline on the clifftop, the description which follows emphasises calmness and tranquillity: desire has gone from Mathias as he remembers, and the scene ends with the phrase, 'Mathias boit tranquillement le reste du café au lait dans son bol' (p.246). As before, the cinema poster provides a commentary on Mathias's state of mind, and now it is blank (p.250).

The reader, it can be seen, has a considerable amount of material to work on for a portrait of Mathias, and no lack of freedom: his role is both interpretive and creative. Robbe-Grillet has provided evidence which it is difficult to ignore, and the reader can hardly escape the conclusion that Mathias has a disordered personality. It is easy to accept the image of Mathias not only as a sexual obsessive, but as a man who is anxious, ineffectual in business (he is in danger of losing his job because of poor performance) and easily dominated (Robbe-Grillet repeatedly notes that Mathias lowers his gaze when in conversation). This picture of inadequacy is, of course, the generalised picture, and in order to progress further the reader must adopt his creative role. The author has made no attempt to indicate the weight and importance to be attached to the diverse elements within Mathias's character, or how they are to be related one to another. The reader must decide: he must fashion his own portrait of Mathias and create, out of the details offered to him, a character who satisfies him. Jean Alter's reference to 'la nature insaisissable de son caractère' is amply justified, and points to the intriguing paradox that Mathias is both present in the text and absent from it. Mathias dominates the novel, whether it is his voice the reader hears or that of another narrator. His vision, one of powerful intensity, is of paramount importance and the reader is given direct access to it. Yet nowhere does Mathias exist as a clearly defined 'character', and because his vision is one which deforms and obscures, because it destroys time and space in its workings, he remains a force of disorder and uncertainty, as well as a fascinating and elusive figure.

7. *Le Voyeur:* Time and Space — Techniques of Narration and Description

If *Le Voyeur* retains at its centre an essential ambivalence — that is, if it presents not a finely shaped narrative with easily identifiable characters, motives and events, but an amalgam of elements whose interrelation is shifting and indeterminate — it is, of course, because Robbe-Grillet wishes it to be so. In his second novel, as in his first, he is undermining the traditional supports of the 'well-made' novel and calling into question the relationship between the novel and the 'real' world outside it. As before, characters, motives and events are not absent, but they lack the authority of formal completeness, and the reader, an accomplice of the author rather than a spectator, is called upon to respond not passively but actively, finding before him a piece of fiction which is fluid and dynamic. Robbe-Grillet has deliberately withheld information not in order to offer his reader the prospect of a laborious search for a cunningly concealed 'truth' — what 'really' happened — but in order to deflect his attention towards other matters. *Le Voyeur*, like *Les Gommes*, is in part an enquiry into the art of writing a novel, and more specifically an enquiry into how far the novel can liberate itself from its traditional function of 'telling a story' and with what it might replace that function. Because the centre of *Le Voyeur* is a void (as the crime is not directly described) and because there is no voice to interpret and categorise the mental processes of Mathias — in other words, because there is no clear reality exterior to the elements within the novel against which those elements may be measured — the reader is forced to consider the text in front of him as complete in itself. He becomes aware of its shape and structure, its juxtapositions, variations and repetitions; the novel becomes a construct, independent of any function as the reproduction of 'reality'. The reader may well feel that Mathias is 'abnormal' because his conduct does not match up to the reader's preconceived notion of what constitutes normal

behaviour, and in that sense the novel's links with the 'real'
world have not been broken; Robbe-Grillet clearly relies upon
the reader's skill in recognising sexual obsessiveness, a skill
unlikely to be developed elsewhere than in contact with the 'real'
world. But the 'normal' is not introduced directly into the novel,
and there is no use made of a narrator to point out what stan-
dards of judgement are to be applied. What remains before the
reader is not comment and analysis, but the vivid immediacy of
images, and the life and movement of *Le Voyeur* are communicated not by the unfolding of a case history but by the patterns and rhythms of the text.

As in *Les Gommes*, the reader is warned in the text itself that
he is not reading a traditional novel where everything will be put
in its proper place and made clear in the end. Comments by the
author are again oblique and ironic; he adopts a wryly dismissive
tone, as if he were aware that the reader might have expectations
which were being frustrated. Robbe-Grillet seems to
acknowledge the difficulties ('Autour de lui, l'état des choses ne
fournissait aucun repère', p.144), and Jean Robin's account of
Jacqueline's misdemeanours could well be that of a bemused
reader of *Le Voyeur*: 'Au lieu de la narration précise d'un
quelconque fait, limité et précis, il n'y eut — comme d'habitude
— que des allusions très embrouillées à des éléments d'ordre
psychologique ou moral, noyés au milieu d'interminables
chaînes de conséquences et de causes, où la responsabilité des
protagonistes se perdait' (p.146). A little later the fisherman's
words again take on characteristics which an unsympathetic
reader might attribute to the novel he is reading: 'Malgré cela
l'ensemble du discours conservait — en apparence du moins —
une architecture cohérente, si bien qu'il suffisait de l'écouter
d'une oreille distraite pour ne pas s'apercevoir des anomalies
qu'il présentait' (p.152). On more than one occasion Robbe-
Grillet points out that it is not he, the author, who will have to
make judgements: the phrase 'Vous allez juger vous-même', a
phrase which comes easily to the lips of a salesman, is also a
direct statement to the reader, who is further reminded that
there are many possible ways of responding to the material
before him: on page 60, for example, the expression on the face

of the girl in the café can be interpreted in a variety of ways. Robbe-Grillet playfully accepts that all is not easy in the art of writing, or reading, novels: not only does Mathias's comment on the slowness of the ferry's manoeuvre, 'Toute cette arrivée était interminable' (p.39), become the comment of an impatient reader, but Mathias becomes a representative of the novelist. After spending too long in unproductive activity, Mathias gets down to business again: 'Mais il n'avait déjà que trop perdu de temps..., il revint à la ligne des façades et à l'exercice incertain de sa profession' (p.69). The last phrase would seem to be spoken with Robbe-Grillet's voice.

As before, there is nothing here which amounts to much in the way of literary criticism, rather a series of warnings to the reader not to approach this novel in the expectation of finding something formally complete. The very title of the novel reinforces a sense of uncertainty. To whom does the word *voyeur* refer? Is it to Mathias, whose fantasies and obsessions are presented in such striking pictorial terms and who 'sees' much in so vivid a way? After all, the word does have sexual overtones which fit in well with Mathias's state of mind. Does it refer to the young Julien, who is apparently a witness to the crime and who is content to watch it without intervening and without reporting it? Does it refer to the reader, who is presented with images appealing to his mind's eye? The *voyeur* may be any one or all three — a conclusion which points to the undesirability of any attempt to limit the novel to a single meaning or series of significances. Robbe-Grillet further emphasises such undesirability by introducing, albeit briefly, a legend (on page 221) to suggest another level of meaning. In the manner of the Oedipus story in *Les Gommes*, this legend offers a pattern into which the elements of the novel might fit. The tone here is somewhat mocking and certainly unreliable, for it is a legend which Mathias has never heard before, although he is constantly aware of other stories from his past which have been told to him.

Everything, then, comes together in *Le Voyeur* to conspire against a feeling of finality and certainty, and in the text 'form' is not at the service of 'content'. As in *Les Gommes*, Robbe-Grillet is interested less in having something to say than in having a manner of saying. He is asking the same questions as before; he is once again experimenting with the possibilities of writing a novel from nothing and about nothing, where the development of the text *as text* becomes a major concern. To this effect he uses techniques which run counter to traditional realism, and the reader finds himself confronted not only with an absence of psychological analysis and the all-seeing eye of the omniscient narrator, but also with the outward signs of Robbe-Grillet *chosiste* and a novel which exploits to a considerable degree the striking and sometimes disturbing effects of repetition and variation.

Robbe-Grillet *chosiste* appears throughout *Le Voyeur*, but particularly notably in the second half of the novel, where he presents a series of scenes in which objects are described carefully, even minutely, in terms either of their surface appearance or of their spatial relationships. Notable examples are those of the objects in the ironmonger's window (p.54), glasses in the café bar (p.123), the *borne kilométrique* (p.191) and the buoy floating in the harbour (p.255). Robbe-Grillet displays his liking for geometric precision; for example: 'C'était une borne kilométrique du modèle ordinaire, parallélépipède rectangle raccordé à un demi-cylindre de même épaisseur (et d'axe horizontal)' (p.191). Another example is that of the bedroom Mathias occupies, which becomes (on page 174) an account of the furniture in it, listed as the pieces are arranged, anticlockwise from the window. On other occasions Robbe-Grillet describes Jean Robin's room, where particular attention is paid to the oil-lamp and to the planes, surfaces and axes which the scene represents (p.223), a seagull (p.231) and the pattern of raindrops on a window (p.232). The effect is disturbing. Amid the fluctuating intensity of Mathias's inner experience, where reality is distorted by the imposition of his vision, there appear moments of calm and stillness, where the descriptions on the page take on an apparently 'neutral' aspect. The *borne*, the buoy, the objects in a room have an undeniable presence, a solidity affirmed by the precision of the language. The reader is reminded once again that for Robbe-Grillet the world has no significance; it merely exists. He is also reminded that there is no complicity between objects and men; objects do not possess any human qualities and cannot be used to provide a comfortable context for character analysis.

Jean-Paul Sartre had already shown the insistent and threatening presence of objects in the world, but that world is characterised ultimately by contingency. Roquentin, in *La Nausée*, had come to realise that there was not simply an absence of order and meaning, but of justification as well: there was no reason why the world should exist in the form it does, or indeed why it should exist at all. The objects in Robbe-Grillet's world exist clearly and precisely, with a striking sense of definite order, order which contrasts forcibly with the disorder which human activity brings. This is notable at the very beginning of *Les Gommes* and throughout *Le Voyeur*.

The context of *Le Voyeur* is, as we have seen, not a fanciful, unreal location, but a specific one, and, moreover, the island, with its cliffs and surrounding sea, is, like the city of *Les Gommes*, an enclosed place. Mathias is kept in, forced to act in a confined space which stands firm and limiting, as an ironic counterpart to the confusion which characterises his actions. The island is not of course described in exhaustive detail, but only in function of Mathias's perception: it exists to emphasise the particularly human, unreliable nature of that perception. Mathias, like Wallas, is uncertain as to locations, directions, topographical dispositions, and the setting in which he finds himself is to him elusive and deceptive. Robbe-Grillet qualifies Mathias's vision of the world with hypothetical and restrictive formulae such as *peut-être*, *vraisemblablement*, *sans doute* and so on, not to place in doubt the authenticity of the thing perceived, but the authenticity of the perception.

Robbe-Grillet is again playing a double game, for the description of objects, as well as emphasising the distance between them and men, is closely interwoven with the inner world of Mathias. Firstly, objects, while imposing themselves upon him, offer him no comfort, but merely turn him back upon himself. They resist his gaze, they yield up nothing of themselves. Because objects which surround him have no meaning, they push him more deeply into his world of fantasy and sexual obsession, and in this sense provide a backcloth for the principal drama. The apparent neutrality of the descriptions offers moments of respite to balance the moments of disorder. But secondly, there are objects which are not only perceived but deformed by Mathias, and which assume their role as supports or reflections of his passions. When he turns his attention to objects and scenes which affect him more immediately, the narrative is full not of planes and surfaces, but textures and colours, and is charged with sensual overtones. Objects become 'contaminated': as with Wallas in *Les Gommes*, and in fact in a more intricate way, Mathias's inner film is presented as the only clue to his mental processes, and that film exists in terms of objects. What is important is the selectivity of Mathias, the particular objects his mind dwells on and his arrangement of those objects. Beds, lamps, cigarette packets, pieces of string, the figure 8 — these are introduced and reintroduced in different combinations and relationships to form a complex network of visual signs. The reader's eye and ear become accustomed to the currents which these controlled repetitions and variations bring, currents which serve not only to suggest an obsessive mind, but which are also used to provide a cohesiveness and unity in literary terms.

Such cohesiveness and unity are of the greatest importance to Robbe-Grillet, and he seeks to achieve them not only by the use of the sort of network referred to above, but also by other means, some of which are all too obvious. Certain phrases are used frequently, such as 'la dernière maison à la sortie du bourg sur la route du grand phare', when describing the Leduc house, or 'on lui avait souvent raconté cette histoire', when reference is made to Mathias's past. Repeated use is made of such phrases as 'une fois, deux fois, trois fois' or 'belle fille', 'belle machine' or 'belle affiche'. Mathias knocks on doors, using his large ring, and opens and closes his samples case countless times. Jacqueline is often referred to as 'un vrai démon', and comments on her on page 170 are taken from earlier scenes. Similarly, the figures of the three fishermen, with their conversation providing an indistinct commentary on Mathias's situation, recur at various moments (for example, on pages 56, 124 and 171). On occasion, the repetitions are less obvious, even playful:

the design on a box of cutting tools in the ironmonger's window, 'en i grec' (p.55), is similar not only to a mark on Violette's leg (p.133), suggesting a reason why Mathias pays particular attention to the tools, but also to a crab's shell (p.144).

Repetition and variation, however unsubtle or however oblique, are Robbe-Grillet's means of directing the reader's attention to the text of *Le Voyeur* as text and of accentuating the blurring between the 'real' and the 'imagined'. As Mathias prepares to leave the ferry as it arrives at the island, he constructs in his mind (on page 35) the scene of an ideal sale (which must last only four minutes). He introduces into it information gained in conversation with the sailor on the mainland (p.32), but when this scene seems unsatisfactory to him, because of the unconvincing way in which the characters behave, he recreates it in different forms (pp.38 and 40), only to be brought back to the present by the sight of the piece of string in the shape of the figure 8 (p.42). Real and imagined are brought together, the distinction between them is abolished, in the same way that chronological time is abolished. Past and present do not exist as separate scales, clearly distinguishable one from the other. On page 231 the scene of Mathias waking in the bedroom is interwoven with the scene from his childhood when he watched the seagull through the rain-flecked window (p.18). The second scene repeats and amplifies details of the earlier scene — the bird itself and the position it adopts, the rain, even 'la table encastrée dans l'embrasure' — so that the reader, who on one level is persuaded that he is confronted with a striking example of Mathias's inability to throw off childhood influences, is made aware of a different level of another recurring pattern, one among many, which bind the novel together. In the closing pages the point is brought forcefully home. On page 253, a description of Mathias's movements, as he opens his case to present his wares, is interrupted; the passage ends with the phrase 'L'extrémité de l'index tendu s'approche du cercle formé par le cadran de la montre fixée à ...'. After a gap on the page, the last few words are repeated, leading into the scene of the arrival of the ferry which Mathias will take back to the mainland. The repeated phrase links two apparently disparate elements, relating one to the other in an unusual way, and suggests that each element is not significant in itself, as a single, irreplaceable event, but as part of a greater whole.

The scene of Mathias's departure which closes the novel recalls the earlier scene of his arrival; there is the same attention paid to the movement of the water, the ship's siren, the details of the harbour wall, and the same comment is passed: 'Il est à l'heure aujourd'hui'. Like *Les Gommes*, *Le Voyeur* comes full circle; time and space, so carefully delineated in the traditional realist novel, have lost their characteristic certainty and authority as reflections of the 'real' world. The opening of the novel can be read as a commentary on the events to be described, and it assumes its full meaning only once the novel has been read: 'C'était comme si personne n'avait entendu. La sirène émit un second sifflement, aigu et prolongé, suivi de trois coups rapides, d'une violence à crever les tympans — violence sans objet, qui demeura sans résultat'. The crime goes not only unpunished, but unheeded — it is as if no-one has heard; and being perhaps the second crime which Mathias has committed, it is the expression of purposeless violence which brings no 'result'. For the reader opening the novel, these references cannot be fully understood; for the reader closing the novel, they show how *Le Voyeur* must be approached without reference to the traditional constraints of meaning, sequence and chronology.

8. Two 'New' Novels?

Robbe-Grillet is known as one of the leading exponents of the *nouveau roman*, and the discussions which have centered around the significance of this term have contributed as much to his fame — or notoriety — as the detailed analysis of his fiction. He has gained a reputation as one of a group writing 'difficult' novels, which break all the known rules and banish humanity, indeed all life, from within their covers. That many novels published in France since the 1950s do differ in tone, structure and style from 'traditional' novels is hardly in dispute; what must be said is that the essential qualities of those novels have often been lost or misunderstood in the rather overheated criticism which they have provoked.

The title *nouveau roman* is, like so many literary labels, more dangerous than helpful. It is a term invented by journalists, for the sake of convenience, to identify a group of authors, including Robbe-Grillet, Butor, Simon, Pinget and Nathalie Sarraute. Members of this group have steadfastly underplayed the common ground which might be seen to exist between them (which, outside a certain superficial level, barely extends beyond the sharing of the same publisher) and have rejected the view that they are all writing novels illustrating similar, preconceived theories. Robbe-Grillet insists that in his eyes the novel is a work of research, and allows only a form of negative union between himself and his contemporaries; in *Le Figaro littéraire* of 26 March 1958, he said: 'Et si un certain nombre de romanciers peuvent être considérés comme formant un groupe, c'est beaucoup plus par les éléments négatifs, ou par les refus qu'ils ont en commun en face du roman traditionnel'.

Comment has already been passed in previous chapters of this study on the way in which this rejection of the traditional novel is expressed in Robbe-Grillet's work. It can be emphasised again here that what he finds impossible to accept is the idea of a narrator who is outside the action but who imposes his vision upon it, a vision which is all-seeing and which offers the reader a privileged insight into something closed and finite. To his own question, 'Qui décrit le monde dans les romans de Balzac?', Robbe-Grillet replies, 'Ça ne peut être qu'un Dieu' (*1*, p.118), and those novels seem to him to offer a false realism and a false omniscience, false in that the point of view they offer does not correspond to any human view. The novel, for Robbe-Grillet, must be more open; it must seek not to limit and define, but to discover new horizons, and he was moved to pass a sharp comment on Sartre as a novelist; in a speech delivered at the University of Keele in February 1960, he said: 'Sartre connaissait la signification de ses livres. Il savait ce qu'il avait à dire. Et c'est ça seulement qui l'a empêché d'être un écrivain'.

Given such a slighting reference, it is hardly surprising that Robbe-Grillet should quickly dismiss moral and political involvement — *engagement* — in the part of the novelist. He feels that for the novelist (or indeed for any artist), despite what may be the firmest of political convictions or sympathy for a militant course of action, art can in no way be reduced to the status of a tool serving a cause, no matter how just that cause might be. The artist can place nothing over and above his work, which is created for no ends beyond itself, and any external pressure or directive, any element of didacticism however slight, indeed any concern for *meaning* is injurious to that work. The only problems to be dealt with are those of art. Here is a straightforward expression of the view that any thesis or philosophy will deform the work of art. The more important a novel's 'message' is seen to be, the more what is properly artistic in that novel will stand in danger of being lost. Robbe-Grillet insists that for the artist art remains of the greatest importance. The traditional divisions between 'form' and 'content' are meaningless, and the two cannot be separated: 'Parler du contenu d'un roman comme d'une chose indépendante de sa forme, cela revient à rayer le genre entier du domaine de l'art. Car l'oeuvre d'art ne contient rien, au sens strict du terme' (*1*, p.42).

Robbe-Grillet's novels, then, stand squarely against the committed novels of the 1930s and 1940s in France. The reader is aware from the first page that he is in a different context from that which informs the work of, for example, Malraux, Saint-Exupéry, Sartre and Camus. These novelists had wished to come to terms with man's situation in the world, which they expressed in philosophical, moral and political terms. They sought to understand the reality of the human condition, and to arrive at values by which life might justifiably be lived. As they did so, they retained the language and the perspective of rational analysis, and sought to persuade their readers by demonstration and illustration, underpinned by a coherent view of man and the world. Literary creation was an act of commitment, a gesture made towards the search for order, meaning and happiness in a world which denied them; the novelist was bound not to remain a passive spectator, but to intervene and act. Robbe-Grillet accepts that he lives in an age when the relationship between man and the world is of primary significance; interest has shifted away from the successes or misfortunes of particular individuals in a carefully drawn social context, and the novels of Balzac not only describe a society which has disappeared: they do not reflect the uncertainties and questionings which are characteristic of an age of scepticism. Yet his dissatisfaction with Balzac's world does not lead him to accept any more readily the world of Sartre or Camus. He urges the rejection of the old traditions of humanism which seek to bind him to the world and involve him in some form of transcendental metaphysics. The recognition that the world exists and nothing more, that it is neither meaningful nor absurd, is the first step man must take along the path which man must tread without recourse to metaphysics.

Robbe-Grillet himself does not seem anxious to tread that path. He is much more concerned with the ways in which he might foster change in the novel's traditional role and transform its contents, to use John Sturrock's phraseology, from 'gratuitous references to the real world' to 'the necessary sequence of a fictive one' (*21*, p.170). He will deal with a reality created in his novels which is distinct from the reality in the midst of which he and his readers live. The cornerstone of that reality will be the image, and the image, as the expression of what the eye sees and what the mind imagines, can be, at different moments, dramatic, evocative, precise or elusive. Above all it has great immediacy, and Robbe-Grillet seeks to make the images he uses compelling, and to capitalise upon the visual sense of the reader. As he put it, 'Je crois que tout ce que l'homme ressent est supporté à chaque instant par des formes matérielles de ce monde. Le désir qu'un enfant a d'une bicyclette c'est déjà l'image nickelée des roues et du guidon. La peur qu'un automobiliste a éprouvée à un croisement conservera toujours la forme d'un capot noir surgi tout à coup avec le buit des freins qui crissent et le paysage qui bascule dans la glace' (*14*, p.222). It is not insignificant that Robbe-Grillet should have turned to the cinema, which he found the ideal medium for the capturing of the mental processes of individuals by exteriorising them onto objects. In an introduction to what remains his most famous film, *L'Année dernière à Marienbad*, he wrote: 'La caractéristique essentielle de l'image est sa présence [...] de toute évidence, ce que l'on voit sur l'écran *est en train de se passer*, c'est le geste même qu'on nous donne, et non pas un rapport sur lui'.

That immediacy and clarity of the image are qualities essential to Robbe-Grillet's fiction, and help to give the two novels under consideration their particular atmosphere, an atmosphere which is strange, challenging and often disquieting. Jean Alter, emphasising Robbe-Grillet's ability to draw pictures and create scenes which are striking because of their vivid, static nature, makes the interesting point that the author paints the world in the manner of Poussin rather than of the Impressionists, or in the style of Braque rather than of the Surrealists. He adds: 'On a souvent comparé le style de Robbe-Grillet à la technique cinématographique; il conviendrait mieux de parler de la lanterne magique, ou du dessin d'une bande animée, avec sa suite de petits tableaux indépendants et achevés, tout prêts à être amplifiés en grandes toiles du *pop art*' (*2*, p.93). Alter sees the tendency of Robbe-Grillet's novels to capture a timeless, essential order in the world: '... ses sujets inanimés témoignent d'une composition presque classique qui transmet ce qui *est* plutôt que ce qui *devient*, une perfection statique plutôt qu'un mouvement à surprises. La précision géométrique et l'indifférence des mots neutres arrachent les objets à l'instabilité du temps et les figent dans des états essentiels' (2, p.93).

Alter is describing here one important element in Robbe-Grillet's fiction, but in so doing he leaves other questions unanswered, for one must not lose sight of what is ephemeral, unstable and particularly human in the novels. Robbe-Grillet, for all his mistrust of explanatory psychology, for all his refusal to write case-histories, introduces characters who have their fair share of weaknesses, uncertainties and passions. *Les Gommes* and *Le Voyeur* contain within them a certain tension, between the static and the dynamic, the timeless and the transitory, the ordered and the disordered, and it is a tension which is made all the more real and all the more disturbing to the reader by the absence of those signposts and directions which he might normally expect.

The tension is increased because a certain kind of duel is being played out between novelist and reader. The reader will tend instinctively to bring the information he has at his disposal into a context of logic and rationality; he will seek to arrange the elements within the novel into a familiar world of cause and effect and chronological time. The novelist challenges the reader to forego this type of reading, which expects the novel to be referential, and to concentrate upon the rhythms and patterns of the text and to see it as a fiction independent of the 'real' world. Robbe-Grillet's novels in this way address themselves to the problem of reading as well as to the problem of writing. In effect, they operate a reversal of traditional values: where once the novelist's art consisted in concealing or effacing the process of its production, the means by which it sought to achieve its ends, so that the illusion of 'reality' could be more effectively accomplished, with Robbe-Grillet that process and those means are brought into the foreground. What is being said is replaced as the chief area of interest by the way in which it is being said. The reader is caught between the natural desire to 'retrieve' the text, and the awareness that any 'retrieval' is at best uncertain and at worst a profound corruption of the text.

Stephen Heath notes the way in which Robbe-Grillet introduces into his novels the idea of 'unreadability' (in the sense of 'unreadability according to traditional expectations', a lack of concern with 'subject-matter' or 'content') (*11*, p.131), and cites the example of the letter that Wallas and Laurent in *Les Gommes* are unable to decipher:

> 'notons qu'un mot est illisible dans une des phrases con-
> sidérées par vous comme significatives — un mot de sept
> ou huit jambages, qui ressemble à ''ellipse'' ou ''éclipse''
> et qui peut aussi bien être ''aligne'', ''échope'', ''idem'' ou
> encore beaucoup d'autres choses.' (p.170)

Heath's commentary on this passage is ingenious:

> The writing aligns (*aligne*) in the line of its progression, but
> is elliptical (*ellipse*) in its play of repetition (*idem*) and dif-
> ference (*ou encore beaucoup d'autres choses*); an elliptical
> alignment that is the instrument of the cutting away of
> sense (*échoppe*), so ending in an eclipse (*éclipse*), a mo-
> ment of dark unreadability... (*11*, p.132)

Faced with this unreadability, the reader, in Heath's terms, 'is called upon to respond to the experience of reading, to the con-struction of the text ('une construction permanente'), to concern himself not with the reception of a message but to assist in a reflection on the structuration of a message, '*un roman lui-même* qui se pense' (*11*, p.133). In order to render this process of reflection more productive and more stimulating, Robbe-Grillet deliberately, and ironically, exploits the attractions of the realistic setting, but subverts that setting to his own ends. The detective story, the 'psychological thriller', the Oedipus myth, complete with its Freudian implications, sexual obsession — all of which are suitable material for any number of traditional novels — become the material for a process of reassembly: what might have constituted a conventional narrative is rearranged in-to a construct characterised not by its fidelity to something ex-ternal to it, but by the internal interdependence of its various elements. The reader discovers that what no longer makes sense on the level of a realistic reading makes sense on the level of the text.

Robbe-Grillet is, therefore, aiming at a self-sufficiency in his novels, and that is nowhere better expressed than in their cir-cularity. Both *Les Gommes* and *Le Voyeur*, as we have seen, have opening and closing scenes which, if they are not identical reflections one of the other, are close parallels. Linear progression and chronological time are denied, not only by devices which we have already noted, but also by the way the novels end where they begin. Modifications, it would appear, have been made: a man has died of a gunshot wound and a young girl has been assaulted and killed, but these modifications are rendered all the more uncertain by the echo of the opening situation on the closing pages, reappearing to mock again the reader tempted to apply realistic criteria to his reading. Events, which in a traditional novel would be seen as certainties, giving the novel its forward movement, are, with Robbe-Grillet, deprived of their central significance. It is as if the novel is turning in upon itself: there is a sense of returning to the point of departure, and a feeling of order is restored after the intervening disorder. But it is not order which follows events explained and behaviour analysed; it is the order of the text complete, whole and unified. Robbe-Grillet makes the point through the structure and also through the imagery. The insistent examples in the novels of images of completeness — the Boulevard Circulaire, the contours of the island, circles, the figure 8, the circularity of time — together with the images of repetition — the identical meals in the self-service restaurant, the reflections of the café proprietor, the superimposing of the figure of Jacqueline upon that of Violette — all these are further echoes of the structure of the novels and reminders of their self-sufficiency.

In his testing and challenging of the reader Robbe-Grillet, of course, has the upper hand, because he still exercises editorial authority; however far removed he appears to be from the actual scene, he is still at work, selecting and arranging. He has written these novels to carefully conceived plans and thus cannot fail to impose some meaning on them; he has chosen the experiences which his characters must face. Robbe-Grillet's predilections are often apparent, and leave a clear mark on his work: one cannot miss his liking for the detective story or thriller, with its atmosphere of ambiguity and its element of suspense, or his interest in the human mind under stress. His early training as a scientist (more precisely, as an agricultural economist) finds expression in the meticulous measurements of planes, surfaces,

angles and distances, a somewhat incongruous counterbalance,
perhaps, to the eroticism with which the novels are suffused.
The reader, in his free response to the texts before him, is faced
not only with the keen intelligence of an author enquiring into
the scope of the novel, but also with that author's personal
idiosyncracies and the particular bent of his imagination.

To what extent, then, are these novels 'new'? Critics have
been anxious not only to situate Robbe-Grillet firmly in the context of the *nouveau roman*, but also to identify literary influences upon him. This exercise, uncertain at the best of times,
is notably difficult in this case and has served only to divide
opinion. Robbe-Grillet himself is not given to mentioning
names, but, acknowledging that the important task of undermining the traditional novel has been a gradual process, does
cite Proust, Faulkner and Beckett (*1*, p.32). To this list other
names have been added by critics, in particular Joyce and
Kafka. Stoltzfus follows up Robbe-Grillet's reference to
Faulkner, and adds an illuminating comment: '*Les Gommes*
emerges as a formal imitation of *Sanctuary* following Malraux's
famous statement in the preface to the 1933 French translation:
"*Sanctuaire*, c'est l'intrusion de la tragédie grecque dans le
roman policier"' (*20*, p.504). On a different level both *Les
Gommes* and *Le Voyeur* clearly draw heavily upon the traditions
of the detective story and the thriller: *Les Gommes* has been seen
by many as a stylish variant on the detective story where the
detective is revealed as the murderer, the most famous example
of which is perhaps Agatha Christie's *The Murder of Roger
Ackroyd*. Although it rejects the formal qualities of the conventional psychological novel, *Le Voyeur* is clearly rich in
possibilities of psychological interpretations, and becomes a
novel of great power. The search for literary precedents,
however, does not do Robbe-Grillet full justice. He is aware of
the traditions and the achievements of prose fiction, however
anxious he appears to be to deny them, and he uses his reader's
familiarity with those traditions to his own advantage. As we
have suggested before, Robbe-Grillet's fiction rests upon tension
and ambivalence, and the two novels under discussion do look
to the future, but have not altogether thrown off the past. The

fact that they stand on a threshold renders them even more intriguing, and Robbe-Grillet's own comment on them catches perfectly the interest they hold for the reader:

... je ferai remarquer que *Les Gommes* ou *Le Voyeur* comportent l'un comme l'autre une trame, une "action", des plus facilement discernables, riche par surcroît d'éléments considérés en général comme dramatiques. S'ils ont au début semblé désamorcés à certains lecteurs, n'est-ce pas simplement que le mouvement de l'écriture y est plus important que celui des passions et des crimes? (*1*, p.38)

Select Bibliography

This select bibliography lists only those critical works which have been of direct use in the preparation of this study. For further details the reader should consult: D.W. Fraizer, *Alain Robbe-Grillet. An annotated bibliography of critical studies 1953-1972* (Scarecrow Author Bibliographies, 13) 1973.

1. Alain Robbe-Grillet, *Pour un nouveau roman*, Paris, Editions de Minuit, 1963

2. J. Alter, *La Vision du monde d'Alain Robbe-Grillet*, Geneva, Droz, 1966

3. C. Audry, 'La Caméra d'Alain Robbe-Grillet', *Revue des Lettres Modernes*, V, nos 36-38 (été 1958), pp.259-69

4. H.E. Barnes, 'The Ins and Outs of Alain Robbe-Grillet', *Chicago Review*, XV (1962), pp.21-43

5. O. Bernal, *Alain Robbe-Grillet: le roman de l'absence*, Paris, Gallimard, 1964

6. L. Bersani, 'Murder French Style', *Partisan Review*, XXXII, 2 (Spring 1965), pp.305-10

7. M. Blanchot, 'Notes sur un roman', *NNRF*, III, 31 (juillet 1955), pp.105-12

8. D. Dreyfus, 'Vraies et fausses énigmes', *Mercure de France*, 1130 (octobre 1957), pp.268-85

9. G. Durozoi, *Robbe-Grillet, Les Gommes*, Paris, Hatier (Profil d'une œuvre), 1973

10. Esprit, 'Le Nouveau Roman', numéro spécial, juillet-août 1958

11. S. Heath, *The Nouveau Roman*, London Elek, 1972

12. V. Minogue, 'The Workings of Fiction in *Les Gommes*', *Modern Language Review*, LVII, 3 (July 1967), pp.430-42

13. B. Morrissette, *Les Romans de Robbe-Grillet*, Paris, Editions de Minuit, 1963

14. M. Raimond, *Le Roman depuis la Révolution*, Paris, Colin (Collection 'U'), 1967

15. E. Rault, *Théorie et expérience romanesque chez Robbe-Grillet: Le Voyeur*, Paris, La Pensée Universelle, 1975

16. L.S. Roudiez, 'The Embattled Myths', in F. Will (ed.), *Hereditas. Seven Essays on the Modern Experience of the Classical*, Austin, University of Texas Press, 1964, pp.75-94

17. ——. *French Fiction Today: a New Direction*, New Brunswick, Rutgers University Press, 1972

18. J.-L. Seylaz, *La Quintefeuille. Cinq études sur Balzac, Nerval, Flaubert, Malraux et Robbe-Grillet*, Lausanne, Coopérative Rencontre, 1974

19. B.F. Stoltzfus, *Alain Robbe-Grillet and the New French Novel*, Carbondale, Southern Illinois University Press, 1964

20. ——. 'A Novel of Objective Subjectivity: *Le Voyeur*', *PMLA*, LXXVII (1962), pp.499-507

21. J. Sturrock, *The French New Novel*, London, Oxford University Press, 1969

22. R. Weil-Malherbe, '*Le Voyeur* de Robbe-Grillet: un cas d'épilepsie psycho-moteur', *French Review*, XXXVIII, 4 (February 1965), pp.469-76

23. S.S. Weiner, 'A Look at Techniques and Meanings in Robbe-Grillet's *Voyeur*', *Modern Language Quarterly*, XXIII (1962), pp.217-24